Intervention Annotated Teacher's Edition

Marsha Roit
Marcy Stein

Level 3

A Division of The McGraw·Hill Companies

Columbus, Ohio

www.sra4kids.com

SRA/McGraw-Hill

A Division of The McGraw-Hill Companies

2005 Imprint

Send all inquiries to:
SRA/McGraw-Hill
8787 Orion Place
Columbus, OH 43240-4027

Printed in the United States of America.

ISBN 0-07-571910-X

4 5 6 7 8 9 QPD 06 05 04

Table of Contents

Worksheets

Casper and Chip

by Carolyn Crimi

illustrated by Kersti Frigell

Once upon a time there was an old peddler
named Casper. He was very poor, but he had a
grand donkey called Chip. Casper loved Chip
very much.

One day, on the way home, Casper and Chip
stumbled upon a pot of silver in a ditch by the
path. "Look, Chip!" said Casper, looking at
the silver.

"This silver will make me a rich man!"

Casper put the silver in Chip's bag and went on.

In a little bit, Casper and Chip stumbled upon a
silver rock as big as a man's hat. "Look, Chip!" said
Casper. "This rock will make me a rich man!"

Casper put the rock in Chip's bag. The rock was
heavy. Poor Chip plodded along.

A little later, Casper and Chip stumbled upon a
solid silver box. "Look, Chip!" said Casper. "This
box will make me a rich man!"

Casper lifted the box onto Chip's back. But the
box was too heavy. Poor Chip fell to the ground.

"Get up, Chip!" cried Casper. "We must cross
the river to get this silver home!" But Chip could
not get up. Casper took the pot of silver out of
Chip's bag.

"There, Chip!" said Casper. "Now can you get up?"

Chip still could not get up. Casper took the silver rock out of his bag.

"There, Chip!" said Casper. "Now can you get up?"

Chip still did not get up. Casper took the silver box off his back.

"There, Chip!" said Casper. "There is nothing left on your back. I will help you get up."

Chip got up. Then Chip and Casper crossed the river to home.

"Well, Chip," said Casper. "We have no silver, but I'd much rather be a poor man with you than a rich man without you!"

The Red and Black Cap

by Caitlin McLeary

illustrated by Len Epstein

"Oh," said Mr. Kam, "a red and black ball cap!" 22

"Where?" asked Len. 25

"There!" said Mr. Kam. 29

"I see the red and black cap," said Len. 38

"Pat the cap," said Mr. Kam. 44

"The cap is damp. It will mat," said Mr. Kam. 54
"This cap is bad." 58

"Oh!" said Pat. "Can Dan have that ball 66
cap back?" 68

"Let Dan have the cap," said Mr. Kam. 76

"Dan has his cap back!" said Len. 83

"Yes," said Pat. "This is Dan's damp, red and 92
black ball cap." 95

Ben and the Cat

by Lucie Shephard

illustrated by Gary Undercuffler

Ben went to the big pen. There was a little cat in back of the big pen. The cat ran when Ben went to pet him.

When Ben fed him, the cat had a nap in Ben's lap.

"I'll let him eat food from a pan," Ben said.

When Ben went to tend to the pigs, the cat sat on Ben's cap. "Scat, cat," Ben said. But the cat didn't scat.

When Ben went to get the hens, the cat ran after Ben's best hen. "Scat, cat," called Ben. But the cat didn't scat.

When Ben went to lock the pen, the cat ran   115
after a rat, and Ben fell. "Scat, cat," said Ben. But   126
the cat didn't scat.   130

Ben sat on a box next to the cat.   139

Then the cat sat in Ben's lap. "Well," said Ben. "I   150
guess I have a new pet. I'll call you Scat."   160

Phil's Work

by Alvaro Ruiz

illustrated by Gary Undercuffler

Phil and his dad chopped logs with axes. They chopped in the hot sun.

"This is not a lot of fun," Phil said.

Phil wished for other work.

"Just watch, Pop," he said. "I'm going to be rich."

As he chopped thick logs, Phil had a plan for work.

I've got it! Corncob dolls!

When a job plan was wrong, Phil was not mad.   68

"It was an odd plan," he'd say. "Other work will   78
come along."   80

Some of Phil's plans would drop with a plop.   89

But when work hit bottom with a splash, Phil   98
was not upset.   101

"It was an odd plan," he'd say. "Other work will   111
come along."   113

"Just watch, Pop," he'd say. "I'll have a plan that   123
is not odd."   126

"Don't stop your odd plans, Phil," his pop   134
would tell him as he got the ax. "But don't stop   145
chopping logs."   147

I've got it!
I'll help golfers!

Pets in Class

by Chris Meramec

illustrated by Thor Wickstrom

A Class Plan

"My dog has six pups," said Phil. "They are so much fun. They run and tumble. Then they nap in their soft bed."

"Have you met Hip-Hop?" asked Ann. "Hip-Hop is Todd's pet frog."

"Lots of children have fun pets," said Bob.

"Ms. Kent, can we bring pets to class?" asked Phil.

"You can," said Ms. Kent. "But we must plan the things we will do."

"We can help with the plans. We can list the things we must do. Then we can have pets in class," said Pat.

"Pets in class will be lots of fun," said Ann.   112

"I am glad we can make a plan for pets in   123
class!" said Todd.   126

The Pet Day   129

"What did you do in school today?" asked Mom.   138

"Not much," said Bob.   142

"But today you had pets in class. Was it fun?"   152
asked Mom. "What did you do?"   158

"Oh, some stuff," said Bob.   163

"Pat's cat hops the best," said Bob.   170

"You had cats hop and skip in class?" asked   179
Mom. "What else did the cats do?"   186

"Not much," said Bob.   190

"What next?" said Mom.   194

"I got to catch a pup," said Bob.   202

"You had to catch pups?" asked Mom.   209

"Yes. Phil's pups were running and dumping things. Then the dogs ran, too. The dogs ran, the cats were hopping, and the pups hid," said Bob. 216 226 235

"That's too bad!" said Mom. 240

"It was fun!" said Bob. 245

"What else?" asked Mom. 249

"Oh, not much. Todd got his frog back. Frogs do not come back when you ask them to," said Bob. 259 269

"The cats were skipping and hopping. The dogs were rushing at the cats. A bunch of pups ran and hid. A frog got away. What a mess!" said Mom. "I bet there will be no pets in class again!" 277 288 299 308

"That's what Ms. Kent said," said Bob. 315

Zip and Fudge

by Carolyn Crimi

illustrated by Kersti Frigell

Zip and Fudge wanted something to do.

"Let's trick the other animals!" said Zip.

They hid until a turtle crept past. "Oh!" yelled Zip and Fudge. The stunned turtle ducked under a rock.

"That was fun!" said Zip. "Let's do it again!"

Zip and Fudge scared a bird, a caterpillar, a frog, a giraffe, and a rat. Then Zip said, "This is fun, but I want to rest."

Zip and Fudge curled up in a circle. When they got up, it was dark.

"We'd better run back to the stump," said Zip.

Just then, a large monster stepped in front of Zip and Fudge. 111 114

"Did you trick the animals?" thundered the monster. 120 122

"Uh . . . uh . . . ," stammered Zip and Fudge. 128

"You have upset the animals," said the large monster. "Promise that you will not trick them again!" 136 143 145

"Yes, Yes," muttered Zip and Fudge. 151

Zip and Fudge rushed back to the stump. Their fun ended. But the other animals had a long chuckle! 159 168 170

Intervention

Jill's Biggest Wish

by Carlos Molta

illustrated by Kersti Frigell

Jill always played by the big river. She loved to go fishing and swimming. Most of all, Jill loved digging in the sand.

When children visited, Jill said, "You must dig." The other children were not interested.

One day Jill dug up a little bottle. She patted it with a rag.

Then, a little girl was in front of Jill. "Make a wish!" giggled the little girl.

"Are you kidding?" gasped Jill.	82

"Not a bit! Think of a wish!" insisted the	91
little girl.	93

"Well," said Jill, "I wish for a million dollars."	102

"In a jiff!" answered the little girl. She tapped	111
her lip and stared at Jill. But nothing happened.	120

"Wish again," said the little girl. "But think of an	130
important wish."	132

"Well," said Jill, "I wish for a pal who will go	143
digging with me."	146

The little girl tapped her chin. She skipped in a	156
circle, but nothing happened.	160

The little girl kicked the sand. "Granting wishes	168
just isn't what I want to do," she said. "But I do	180
love to dig!" she said with a wink.	188

Jill grinned at her new pal. The little girl had	198
granted her biggest and most important wish.	205

Dave the Brave

by Ana Rojas

illustrated by Len Epstein

"I am the bravest!" Dave said. "Today, I swam across a lake to save a dog."

"But, Dave," said his little sister, Val, "you can't swim."

"I came face-to-face with a big cat in Africa," said Dave.

"But, Dave," said Val, "you are scared of cats."

"I saved a snake from a dragon," said Dave.

"But, Dave," said Val, "you hate snakes."

"I raced a truck on a dirt trail," said Dave.   82

"But, Dave," said Val, "you can't race."   89

Just then a big snake came up to Dave and Val.   100

"I'm afraid of snakes!" said Dave.   106

"Scram, snake, scram!" yelled Val. She chased   113
the snake.   115

"You're brave, Val," said Dave.   120

"Yes, Dave," said Val, "But will I ever be as   130
brave as you?"   133

Sleepy Steve

by Peter Matheny

illustrated by Len Epstein

Sleepy Steve was afraid. He hurried into a big building and hid beneath a heap of sticks.

"I am free!" Steve eeked. "But I am very sleepy! I need a place to sleep!"

Sleepy Steve peeked out from beneath the sticks. "Eeek!" said Steve. He saw big sticks. He saw little sticks. Steve was afraid.

Sleepy Steve began to sneak past the sticks. "Eeek!" said Steve. He saw big feet. He saw little feet.

He leaned back and fell asleep where he was.

When Steve was awake, he came from beneath the sticks. He peeked back at them.

"Please tell me what you are," Steve said to the sticks. But the sticks did not speak.

Then Steve saw a sign near the sticks. 132
"Dinosaur?" said Steve. "These sticks are a 139
large dinosaur!" 141

Steve climbed up the dinosaur and made a 149
neat nest. "Pleased to meet you," whispered 156
Steve. And the two new pals settled into a deep 166
peaceful sleep. 168

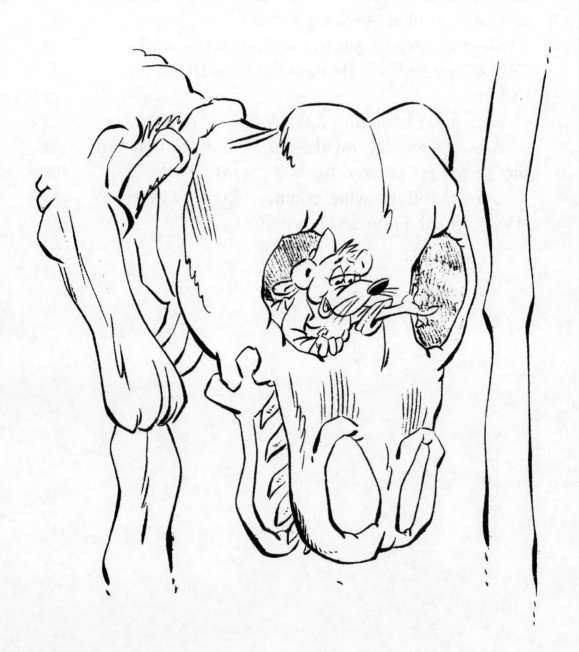

The Shy Bird's Trick

by Wiley

illustrated by Kersti Frigell

Once a sly fox lived deep in the forest. The sly fox was very hungry.

"I might die of hunger!" he cried.

Then, the sly fox spied a bird flying in the sky.

"I will trick this bird," said the sly fox. "It will make a nice pie."

"Oh, shy little bird," called the sly fox. "You look tired. Come and lie on my soft fur."

The bird in the sky didn't say anything.

"Sweet, shy bird," said the sly fox. "I need your help to tie this string on my pie box. Inside is a yummy pie for my mother."

"Is that a lie?" asked the shy bird.

"Oh, no," cried the sly fox as he licked his lips. "I   131
need your help."   134

"I'll bet there is no pie in that box," the shy bird   146
mumbled. "I'll bet that sly fox wants *me* to be the   157
pie!"   158

"I will help you," replied the shy bird. "Hold the   168
string with your long tail while I tie it," she said to 180
the fox.   182

Then, the shy bird tied the fox's tail to the box   193
in a tight knot.   197

"My tail is stuck!" grumbled the fox.   204

"See, fox," sighed the shy bird, "you are sly, but   214
not as sly as I."   219

"Bye-bye, sly fox!" cried the bird, and she flew   228
off into the sky.   232

The Lives of Sea Turtles

by Chris Meramec

illustrated by Diane Blasius

Turtles in the Sea

16

This is a green sea turtle. A sea turtle has
flippers for feet. It flaps its flippers like wings
when it swims. A sea turtle has a shell that makes
swimming easy. The curved top and flat bottom
help to lift the shell, and the turtle can glide
through the sea.

The shell keeps the turtle safe from danger, too.
But a sea turtle cannot pull in its head and legs.
The sea turtle has a very thick skin and scales on
its head and legs.

26
35
46
54
64
67

76
87
98
102

Sea turtles eat and sleep in the sea. The green 112
sea turtle eats tender sea grass that lies on the 122
sandy bottom. It swims to the top to breathe. 131

Turtles do not have teeth, but they do have 140
strong beaks. The beak of a sea turtle can crack 150
shells. Sea turtles might eat shellfish, jellyfish, 157
small sea animals, and wild sea plants. 164

Sea turtles only leave the sea to lay their eggs. 174
A mother turtle digs a nest in the sand. She lays 185
hundreds of eggs in a pile. Then she covers the 195
nest and returns to the sea. The sun keeps the 205
sand and the eggs warm and dry. Mother turtles 214
never see their babies. 218

When the eggs hatch, the shells of the baby 227
turtles are soft. The little turtles must get to the 237
sea. They start to edge across the sand. Danger 246
awaits. Birds circle high in the sky. They eat many 256
of the little turtles. Crabs eat some, too. 264

The baby turtles can swim when they are born. 273
They can even find things to eat. But they are still 284
not safe. Big fish hunt the soft little turtles. 293

Hundreds of turtles hatch on the beach. Many 301
will be eaten. Not many will live to be big turtles. 312

At some time they will return to this same 321
beach to lay their eggs. 326

Baby Turtles 328

"Papa!" yelled Carlos. "Come see the birds. They 336
are everywhere on the beach!" 341

"Turtle eggs must be hatching," said Papa. "The 349
birds are feasting on baby turtles." 355

"Baby turtles! Let's hike down there!" said Carlos. 363

"There are hundreds and hundreds of little 370
turtles!" said Carlos. "See, they are creeping to 378
the sea." 380

"The little turtles try to get to the sea," said 390
Papa. "But it is a hard trip. Their flippers are made 401
for swimming, not for creeping on land." 408

"Their little shells are so soft," said Carlos. 416

"Their shells will get harder as the turtles get 425
bigger," said Papa. 428

"Go away," said Carlos. He waved at the flying 437
gulls. "Let the little turtles get to the sea!" 446

"Even then they may not be safe," said Papa. 455
"Big fish eat the soft little turtles, too." 463

"What will happen to the baby turtles?" 470
asked Carlos. 472

"When they get to the sea, the little turtles will 482
swim as hard as they can for two days. They will 493
not even stop to eat. They may swim as far as 504
Africa," said Papa. 507

"We will never see them again," said Carlos.   515

"Yes, you may," said Papa. "Green sea turtles   523
travel to faraway places like some birds do. But   532
they come back to the beach where they were   541
born to lay their eggs. These turtles will come   550
back to this same beach for as long as they live."   561

"Here, little turtle, swim hard," said Carlos.   568

"You have a long way to go. Stay safe.   577

Please come back to our nice beach."   584

Turtles have lived in the seas for many, many   593
years. Turtles swam in the seas when dinosaurs   601
lived. Those sea turtles were very much like the   610
sea turtles of today.   614

Chinlow of Singboat

by Jo Olson

illustrated by Pat Lucas-Morris

In the little village of Singboat lived a girl named Chinlow. She loved nature. Nature loved her.

The birds of the forest sang more sweetly for her. The doe of the forest ate from her hand. The snows on the hills shone whitest for her.

The roses Chinlow planted would always grow tall.

"Where does Chinlow's talent come from?" people of the village asked. "Even the rainbow is more dazzling over Chinlow's home."

News of Chinlow's talent reached the emperor in faraway Pancoat.

"Could the talent of a simple child overthrow   101
the emperor?" he wondered. "I must not let this   110
go on."   112

The emperor called for his wisest teachers. "I   120
must know," he said, "the talent of Chinlow."   128

One by one the teachers spoke to Chinlow.   136
"Show me," each teacher said.   141

Chinlow looked into the face of a tiny rose. The   151
rose Chinlow looked at began to grow until it   160
became the loveliest rose in the garden.   167

Each teacher said, "I saw her talent, but I do not   178
know it."   180

Finally, the emperor called Chinlow to him.   187
"Show me," he said. Chinlow looked into the   195
face of a tiny rose. The rose grew and became   205
lovely. Then the emperor said to Chinlow, "Now   213
look at me."   216

Chinlow looked into the emperor's eyes. The   223
emperor saw love in her eyes. "Now I know her   233
talent," he said, "and I am not afraid of it. Her   244
talent is love."   247

Mrs. Music

by Carolyn Crimi

illustrated by Anthony Accardo

2

5

9

Every day Mrs. Music and her cat Stu went for a stroll.

"Look!" Mrs. Music said one day to Stu. "Someone has thrown a beautiful dish into the trash! That dish would look grand on my table."

Mrs. Music rushed home and put the dish on her table. The dish was beautiful, but the table was full.

"Stu," said Mrs. Music, "a cleaning is needed! I don't use these candlesticks anymore. I will throw them away."

Hugo was walking home from work when he saw the candlesticks.

"What unusual candlesticks!" he said to himself. "They must have come from a museum. Aunt Iris would love them!"

Hugo picked up the candlesticks and took them to his aunt.

Hugo put the candlesticks on Aunt Iris's shelf.

The candlesticks were beautiful, but the shelf was full.

"Hugo," said Aunt Iris, "a cleaning is needed! I don't use this clock anymore. I have quite a few others. I will throw this one away."

19

21

29

37

46

55

64

66

75

83

85

93

96

103

112

115

123

126

134

141

143

152

162

169

Later that day Mr. Quinlan came by with his 178
cart. "What a beautiful clock!" he cried. "It must be 188
valuable. I will take it home." 194

But Mr. Quinlan's cart was full. "A cleaning is 203
needed," Mr. Quinlan said. "I don't use this bugle 212
anymore. I will throw it away." 218

The next day Mrs. Music and Stu went for 227
their walk. 229

"Oh, my!" said Mrs. Music when she saw the 238
bugle. "Stu, look at that beautiful bugle! I wonder 247
where I can put it?" 252

Root Stew

by Marie Foster

illustrated by Deborah Colvin Borgo

2

5

10

19

29

36

45

48

56

65

75

82

Scooter and Bruce lived in an old boot next to a blue pool. Most of the time, Scooter's and Bruce's lives went smoothly. During the day, they snoozed inside the cool boot. At night, they snooped for food.

The only time Scooter's and Bruce's lives did not go smoothly was when the moon was bright. When the moon was bright, they hid in the boot and listened for Hunter's "Hoot, hoot, hoot."

They knew that "Hoot, hoot, hoot" meant that   90
Hunter was hungry. Mice were not safe when   98
Hunter was hungry.   101

Scooter thought it was his duty to do something   110
about Hunter.   112

"Hunter always seems hungry," he said, "and he   120
always seems to be in a bad mood. Maybe Hunter   130
isn't getting anything nice to eat."   136

The next day, Scooter worked. Into a pot he   145
tossed chopped roots, berries, and shoots. That   152
night, before the moon rose, Scooter crept over to   161
Hunter's roost. There, he left the pot of root stew. 171

As the moon rose, Scooter and Bruce listened.   179
In the distance, they heard Hunter's call. "Hoot,   187
hoot, hoot! Hoot, hoot, hoot!"   192

"Rats!" said Scooter gloomily. "He didn't like the   200
root stew."   202

Hunter flew closer and closer. "He's really in   210
a bad mood tonight," said Bruce. "He must hate   219
root stew!"   221

Scooter listened hard. Then he squeaked with   228
glee! "Why, Hunter isn't calling 'Hoot, hoot,   235
hoot!'" he exclaimed. "Hunter is calling 'Stew,   242
stew, stew!'"   244

A Day in the Amazon

by Dottie Raymer

illustrated by Pat Lucas-Morris

It is a peaceful day in the Amazon. A light breeze shakes the tree leaves.

High above the jungle, a huge eagle watches as the rain forest wakes up. So far, the day seems still.

But the rain forest is never completely quiet. Deep in the jungle, creatures stir. Spider monkeys leap from tree to tree. Their tails grab long vines as they find their way to ripe fruit.

A bird perches in a fig tree. It uses its bright beak to snip off a fig. It throws the fig into the air. It catches the fig in its beak.

Nearby, a giant anteater opens an ant nest. It pokes its long nose into the nest to find its tiny food.

A jaguar slips silently through the trees below. The jaguar's spotted coat hides it well. It stops beside a stream and dips its tail into the water. A fish rises to the bait. Surprise! The jaguar has a tasty meal.

In the trees above, only the three-toed sloth remains quiet. It moves so slowly that mold grows on its fur. The green mold helps it hide in the leaves. The sloth isn't moving at all. The lazy sloth is asleep. When night comes, it will slowly wake to eat.

5
8
12
22
27
36
47
55
63
73
81
92
105
112
120
131
133
141
150
157
164
168
173
177
181
185
190
196
202
206
212
216
222

Hugo Bugle

by Dennis Fertig

illustrated by Robert Byrd

Toast

"Spike, I have a new idea," said Hugo. "It is a faster way to have toast when you wake up."

"At night, tie a shiny pie plate to a wire. Make the wire go to a window. Set a bag of marbles by the window. By the bed, put a few stones."

"Place a tube on the side of the window. Below the tube, glue the blue pail to the end of a pole. Put the pole under the lower window."

"Tie a rope to this side of the window. Tie a heavy ice cube tray to the rope. Use the heaviest one you can find. Load the toaster. Go to bed."

"Wake up to noisy music. Scoop some of the heavier stones into the shiny pie plate. When the shiny plate drops, the window opens."

"When the top window opens, sliding marbles go through the tube. The pail fills, and the pole dives low. Then the lower window pops wide open."

"The heavy ice cube tray hits the right   180
spot. And very soon, up pop the warmest slices   189
of toast."   191

"Tell me the truth, Spike. Is this a cool idea?" 201
asked Hugo.   203

"Oh, my. The idea is nice," said Spike. "But I do 214
not like toast."   217

A New Unit

220

"Joan, you might like my new idea," said Hugo.   229

"I will try," said Joan with a shining smile.   238

"It is a unit that you use to speak to any human,   250
even miles away," said Hugo.   255

"The unit is a huge hat. It has wires, fuses, and   266
tubes. Use the blue tube to speak. To hear, use the   277
white tubes in the holes on the sides."   285

"Right on the top is a light in a red cone. While   297
the light glows, it shows that a special microchip is   307
in use. The microchip changes speech into code."   315

"The code is made of blaring tones from bugle,   324
flute, and tuba music. A spy will not have a clue to   336
what you say. A spy will hear the happiest tune,   346
not a clue."   349

"No matter where you go on the globe, you can   359
easily use the unit. If you tie it on your chin, you   371
can use it when you ride a bike, row a boat, or fly   384
in a plane."   387

"So, Joan, will you try it?" asked Hugo.   395

"No, thanks," said Joan. "I will simply use   403
my phone."   405

Fran's Gift

by Carolyn Crimi

illustrated by Anthony Accardo

Once there was a queen with three girls. Their names were Martha, Greta, and Fran.

"Tomorrow is my birthday," said the queen to the girls. "The girl who finds the smartest and most useful gift will be the next queen."

Martha and Greta worried. "There is a grand party tonight!" they said. "We must get a gift quickly or we will miss the party!"

"The market is close," said Martha. "I will run there and purchase Mother a sparkling cart."

"Martha is smart," thought Greta. "I will run to the market, too. I will buy Mother a marble throne."

The youngest girl, Fran, puzzled over her 115
mother's gift. Finally, she said, "I will knit a scarf 125
with stripes." 127

Fran bought yards of green and blue yarn and 136
started to work. 139

Fran's sisters spoke shrilly to her. "Our gifts are 148
more charming," they said. "You will have to work 157
hard. You will miss the grand party!" 164

Fran knit and knit. By twilight, her arms hurt, 173
but the scarf still wasn't finished. 179

"I will work into the night," she said. 187

Martha and Greta sneered. "Think of missing a 195
grand party for a silly scarf." 201

The next day, the girls took their gifts to 210
the queen. 212

"Here is a sparkling cart," said Martha. "See 220
how it shines!" 223

"This marble throne is the largest in the 231
kingdom!" said Greta. 234

"These gifts are very charming," said the queen, 242
"but I already have a cart and a throne." 251

Then Fran gave the queen her scarf. 258

"This scarf," said the queen, "will keep me 266
warm, and green and blue stripes are charming! 274
You will be a smart queen, Fran." 281

And Fran was. 284

A Book for Mr. Hook

by Carolyn Crimi

illustrated by Kersti Frigell

Once an old man named Mr. Hook lived by a brook in the woods. Whenever the children played by the brook, the old man yelled, "Stay away from my brook!"

"Why does he act like that?" Lucy asked her mother.

Lucy's mother said that Mr. Hook was blind. She took a cloth and tied it across Lucy's eyes. "Here," she said. "Maybe this will help you understand how Mr. Hook feels."

Lucy tried putting on her shoes. She could not even find her foot.

Worst of all, Lucy could not read. "I don't know what I would do if I could not read books!" said Lucy.

Lucy took off the cloth. She went to her bookshelf and chose a book. "This is a good book," she said. "I'll bet Mr. Hook would like it."

Lucy's mother understood. "Good idea!" she said.

Lucy and her mother took the book to Mr. 162
Hook's house. "My teacher said I need to practice 171
reading. May I read my book to you?" 179

"What book?" yelled Mr. Hook. 184

Peter Pan," said Lucy. 188

"Hmm," said Mr. Hook. "Well, okay . . . " 194

Lucy read her book to Mr. Hook every day. One 204
day, the children came to play at the brook. "Why 214
doesn't Mr. Hook yell at us anymore?" they asked 223
Lucy's mother. 225

"He's got a new friend," she said. 232

"Who?" the children asked. 236

"Peter Pan," said Lucy's mother. 241

Taffy for Uncle Warren

by Marie Foster

illustrated by Gary Undercuffler

4

7

11

Uncle Warren was an unhappy man. Every day, he went to the end of the pier to fish. Uncle Warren never got anything. He just sat lonely and unhappy. Everyone thought he was just disagreeable.

Uncle Warren's niece, Marcella, was an unselfish girl. She worried about him. Every day, she watched him on the pier. One chilly, rainy morning Marcella made a decision. She went to the end of the pier.

"Look what I have, Uncle Warren! Taffy! Your favorite candy!" she called. Uncle Warren didn't say anything.

"Have some, Uncle. It tastes wonderful!" said Marcella. Before Uncle Warren could disagree, Marcella popped a piece of the taffy into his mouth. Uncle Warren silently chewed the taffy.

As her uncle ate, Marcella retold a funny story.

"Remember my first piece of taffy?" she asked. "I had a useless tooth that wouldn't come out. You said a good piece of taffy would get my tooth out. You said a good piece of taffy could do anything."

The story made Uncle Warren grin. Marcella hadn't seen him grin in a very long time.

18
29
37
44
46

52
60
69
77
82

90
97
99

106
112
121
128

137

145
155
166
176

183
192

Every day after that, Marcella returned to the   200
pier to give taffy to her uncle.   207

One day, during a really delightful story,   214
Marcella dropped a piece of taffy into the water. A   224
fish snatched the taffy and quickly swam away.   232
Uncle Warren stared at the fish. Then he stuck a   242
piece of taffy onto his fishhook.   248

Uncle Warren tossed the hook and taffy into   256
the water. Suddenly, a fish jumped up and grabbed   265
the hook.   267

"I've got one! I've got one!" yelled Uncle Warren.   276
"At last!"   278

Marcella grinned at her smiling uncle. "Yes!" she   286
said. "A good piece of taffy can do anything!"   295

The Prince's Foolish Wish

by Laura Edwards

illustrated by Linda Kelen

The Prince and the Worm

Walter was a selfish prince. He liked only two things. He liked his dog Pooch, and he liked silver. He had piles and piles of silver. Each night he would lock his treasure room. Each morning he would unlock his treasure room. Then he would stack and restack the piles of silver.

One day Walter was playing with Pooch in the garden. The sunlight sparkled on the water in the pool. This made Walter wonder, "Wouldn't it be wonderful if the pool were filled with silver?"

All of a sudden, Walter heard a splash. He spotted a little worm in the water. He lifted the worm from the pool. Walter was ready to toss the worm away. Suddenly it spoke.

"Don't throw me away," said the worm.

"Why not?" asked Walter. "What is a little worm worth to me?"

The worm said, "I am not worthless. I'm a magic worm. I can grant you three wishes. What do you want?"

"I would like my pool filled with silver," said Walter.

"So it is," said the worm.

When the pool filled with silver, Walter was 200
unable to speak. "I am speechless," he said to 209
the worm. 211

"You have two more wishes," said the worm. 219
"But I must warn you to take care. Be careful what 230
you wish." 232

Walter heard only the words *two more wishes*. 240
The worm's warning was unheard. Walter quickly 247
made a second wish. 251

"I wish that everything I touch would turn to 260
silver," said Walter. 263

"That is not a wise wish," said the worm. 272

"Your job is to grant my wish," said Walter. "You 282
heard what I want." 286

"Your wish is granted," said the worm. "Perhaps 294
you will learn a lesson. Only a fool makes 303
foolish wishes." 305

Walter ran through the garden. He touched 312
chairs, the roses, and the stones on the path. 321
Everything turned to silver. 325

"It works! It works!" cried Walter. "Watch this!" 333
He put his hand under the water. Clink, clink, 342
clink! He heard the silver drip into a pile. 351

"Yes, it works," said the worm. "I will dig into 361
the soft earth. That is where I will be when you 372
need me." 374

"I won't need you," snapped Walter. "I have all 383
the wealth I need. A wealthy prince does not need 393
a worthless little worm." 397

The Foolish Wish 400

Walter rushed into his palace. He put his hand 409
on each thing he spied. Soon he had silver carpets, 419
silver tables, and a silver throne. 425

"I'm hungry," said Walter. "I will have lunch, 433
then I will spend all afternoon turning things 441
to silver." 443

But Walter soon discovered his first problem. 450
Each bite he tried to eat turned to silver. He was 461
unable to eat anything. Soon he had a plate of 471
uneaten silver food. He felt much discomfort. 478

Walter returned to the garden. Pooch had 485
a bone. 487

"Look, Pooch," said Walter. "We can play with a 496
silver bone." 498

Walter picked up the bone. It turned to silver. 507
He tossed the bone across the path. Pooch fetched 516
the bone and returned to Walter. 522

"Nice dog, Pooch," said Walter. He bent over to 531
pet Pooch on the head. In an instant, Pooch froze. 541
Instantly, Pooch turned to silver! 546

"Pooch! Poor Pooch! Worm! Worm! I need you!" 554
cried Walter. 556

The little worm poked its head out of the earth. 566
"How can a worthless worm help a wealthy 574
prince?" asked the worm. 578

"Oh, worm, you were right. I made a foolish 587
wish. I can't eat. I turned poor Pooch to silver. I 598
want to eat. I want Pooch to be furry again. I want 610
to return to the way I was." 617

"You have just one more wish," said the worm. 626
"Do you want to eat? Do you want Pooch back? 636
Try to be wise. Do not make an unwise wish." 646

This time Walter was careful. He stopped to 654
think. Then he said, "I wish that everything would 663
return to the way it was." 669

"Commendable. Your wish is granted," said 675
the worm. 677

"Arf, Arf," said Pooch. 681

Drip, drip, splash, splash went the water. 688

"Let's eat!" said Walter. And he didn't worry 696
over his silver ever again. 701

Flower the Cow

by Dottie Raymer

illustrated by Deborah Colvin Borgo

Once a brown cow named Flower lived on a
farm just outside of town.

Flower stayed mostly out in the field. She kept
her head down, and never seemed to notice the
other animals around the farm.

"How can that cow be so proud?" Howdy the
horse wondered aloud.

"Why, she can't even pull a plow!"

"Pull a plow?" shouted Stout the sow. "That's
nothing to be proud of! However, if she could root
around in the ground with her snout, now that
would be something to be proud of!"

"Root around?" clucked the hens and other
barnyard fowl. "That's nothing to be proud of.
However, if she could lay eggs like ours, now that
would be something to be proud of!"

Finally, little Scooter the mouse spoke up.
"Well, I don't know about plowing, or rooting, or
laying eggs," she said.

"But I do know that you can always count on   163
Flower for just the right amount of sweet milk."   172
    Scooter looked around at the animals. They   179
looked down at the ground.   184
    "It sounds," said the mouse, "like some animals   192
around here are too proud . . . but I doubt that   201
Flower is one of them!"   206

Paul, Aunt Maud, and Claude

by Carolyn Crimi

illustrated by Kersti Frigell

5

8

12

20

28

37

42

49

56

64

71

73

82

84

94

102

109

116

121

Paul's Aunt Maud owned a tiger named Claude. Claude had four big paws with sharp claws.

"Claude is really quite tame," said Aunt Maud. "I have even taught him tricks."

Paul watched as Claude performed his tricks. Claude could turn somersaults. He could balance on a seesaw. He could even do laundry!

"He must be an awfully smart tiger," thought Paul.

"How do you get Claude to do these tricks?" asked Paul.

"I feed him well," said Aunt Maud. "He likes to gnaw on sausages and raw cauliflower, and he loves to sip buttermilk through a straw."

One day Aunt Maud looked distraught. "Claude must be lost!" she said.

"I can help," said Paul.   126

Paul ran across Maud's lawn to a dairy farm.   135
"These cows look awfully scared," thought Paul.   142
"I'll bet Claude has been here."   148

He looked down and saw buttermilk paw prints.   156
He followed them to a nearby store.   163

Outside the store, Paul saw an open box   171
of straws.   173

"Claude must have been here, too!" said Paul.   181
He followed the straws until he came to the   190
playground. There sat Claude on the seesaw.   197

"You must be hungry, Claude," said   203
Paul cautiously.   205

Paul gave Claude some sausage. Then, with a   213
trail of raw cauliflower, he slowly led the tiger   222
back home.   224

"You found him!" said Aunt Maud happily. "You   232
returned my pet tiger!"   236

Aunt Maud gave the exhausted Claude a kiss.   244
Then she turned to Paul. "Now can you help me   254
find my pet lion?"   258

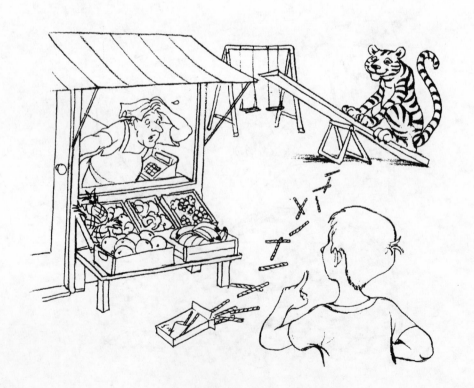

Toy Store Explorer

by Zena Smith

illustrated by Deborah Colvin Borgo

3

6

11

I like to explore Roy's wonderful toy store.

Here's a shiny kite made completely of red, green, yellow, and blue foil. What a spectacular sight that would be in the sky.

Now here's another fine choice. It's a model of a ship. It's a destroyer. Look at all the pieces. I'd need glue to join them all.

Next is an oil truck with a cab and trailer. They come apart. It also has a flexible hose.

19

27

35

42

52

62

68

79

87

There are shelves of dolls. They come in all 96
shapes and sizes. Here's a princess in a royal 105
gown. Another doll has a voice that sounds 113
almost human. 115

There's still so much more to see. There are 124
games, books, jigsaw puzzles, and so many more 132
toys. What can I choose? 137

Well, here is my choice. It's a bright plastic coil 147
that does all kinds of tricks. 153

Rock Collecting

by Carolyn Crimi

illustrated by Gary Undercuffler

2

5

9

20

28

38

46

49

59

69

79

86

94

101

104

112

119

127

136

144

146

Have you ever picked up a rock out of the soil just because you liked the way it looked?

If you like looking at rocks, you might become a rock collector. Rock collectors are people who are curious about rocks.

Rocks are a part of nature. You might find rocks by rivers. You might find them on the beach. You might even find them along a street in a town.

Different kinds of rocks have different features. Some rocks, like limestone, are quite soft. These rocks easily break into powder. Others, like quartzite, are hard.

Rocks with fossils are highly prized by serious collectors. These rocks contain the remains or marks from plants and animals that were alive long ago. Fossils turn up in the most surprising places. Keep your eyes open. You might find one, too!

Rocks are not just for studying. Small rocks can   155
be painted with smiling faces or made to look like   165
tiny mice. Two large rocks might make a nice set   175
of bookends. A giant rock might be just the right   185
size for climbing.   188

So the next time you are walking, you might   197
just find the rock that will make you a rock   207
collector well into the future!   212

Joyce Writes a Good Story

by Carolyn Crimi

illustrated by Meg McLean

A Good Idea

Joyce had to write a story for school. She thought and thought, but she did not know what to write about.

"Why not write about a boy and his toys," said her brother.

Joyce did not want to write about a boy and his toys.

Joyce's sister said, "Why not write about a girl with brown hair and a beautiful voice?"

"That would not be my first choice," said Joyce.

Joyce's father was in the garden watering flowers. Joyce asked him what she should write about.

"You could write about a man and his flowers," said her father.

"No," said Joyce. "That's not good."

Next door, Joyce saw Howard and Shawn playing football on the lawn.

"Have you finished your story?" asked Shawn.

"Not yet," said Joyce.

"You should do it now," said Howard. "We must read them out loud tomorrow."

Joyce found Mom and sat down with a frown.

"Did you think of something to write about?" asked Mom.

Joyce shook her head.

"You should write about the things you know best," said Mom.

5
8
12
15
24
34
36
46
48
58
60
69
76
85
92
99
101
110
113
119
126
131
138
142
151
156
165
173
175
179
187
190

Joyce went for a walk. She walked and talked   199
to herself. She thought about what her mother had   208
said. Suddenly, Joyce had an idea.   214

Joyce ran back to her house as quick as a   224
mouse. She ran past Howard and Shawn on the   233
lawn. She ran past her father. She ran past her   243
sister and her brother.   247

"Where's the fire?" asked Mom.   252

"In my head!" shouted Joyce with joy.   259

Joyce took out her notebook. Her sister entered   267
the room.   269

"What is your story about?" asked her sister.   277

"A girl who does not know what to write   286
about," said Joyce.   289

"Am I in your story?" asked her sister.   297

"Of course!" said Joyce.   301

Joyce in Class   304

"I am afraid to read my story out loud to the   315
class," said Joyce.   318

"Calm down," said Mom. "The class will enjoy   326
your story. But hurry or you will be late for school." 337

Joyce looked for her books. She took her time.   346
She did not care if she was late. She wished she   357
could avoid school today.   361

Joyce caught the school bus. She saw Howard   369
and Shawn.   371

"We know our stories by heart," said Shawn.   379

Joyce felt worse. She wanted to know her story   388
by heart, too. She tried to practice reading it on   398
the bus, but the boys and girls were too noisy.   408

At school, Joyce talked to her friend Soo Lin.   417
"I'm afraid to read my story out loud," she said to   428
Soo Lin.   430

"Me, too!" said Soo Lin. "But I thought I was the 441
only one who was afraid." 446

"I know!" Soo Lin went on. "I'll look at you, and 457
you look at me when we read. Maybe that will help 468
us feel brave." 471

When Joyce stood up to read, her knees shook. 480
She felt awful. She felt awkward. Then she looked 489
at Soo Lin, who was smiling. Joyce felt better. She 499
read her story, and the class applauded. 506

"Your story was really good!" said Soo Lin. 514

"So was yours!" said Joyce. "We don't ever have 523
to be afraid again . . . as long as we are in the same 535
room and can help each other feel brave." 543

Super Kazoo

by Jorge Hernandez

illustrated by Len Epstein

At the Zoo

My name is Drew, and this is the tale of my Super Kazoo.

This is my big brother Stew. He is really cool.

Sometimes when my mom and my dad are too busy, Stew picks me up after school.

Last Tuesday we went to the zoo.

We saw raccoons and baboons running on roofs and splashing in pools.

There were shops that sold all kinds of things like candy and gifts and bright balloons.

We walked and we talked, and soon we were so 96
hot, we had to cool off. 102

So we sat on a stoop and ate two scoops of ice 114
cream with two huge spoons. 119

Out of nowhere, there came a band . . . led by a 129
flute, then a bassoon and then, of all things, a 139
kazoo! 140

The band huffed and puffed some strange kind 148
of tune. 150

The sound of that kazoo was so strange and 159
so new, I knew that I had to have one, too. 170

My Super Kazoo 173

There were so many colors, I just 180
couldn't choose! 182

Red? Green? Blue? 185

I had no clue! I was way too confused. 194

So I closed my eyes tight. I reached in with 204
each hand, first left then right and I pulled out a 215
Super Kazoo. It was not just red or green or blue, 226
but red AND green AND blue! 232

I quickly picked it up and blew. Out flew a 242
sound, not like a duck or a loon, but much more 253
like a moo. 256

I stopped and I waited for everyone to hiss and   266
boo. But they just danced to the kooky sound of   276
my Super Kazoo. Even my big brother Stew got   285
into the groove.   288

On the way home, I blew and I blew. I played   299
such a cool tune that everyone from here to the   309
moon came to dance and salute the sounds of my   319
Super Kazoo.   321

Queen Kit

by Lisa Trumbauer

illustrated by Olivia Cole

Maybe This!

Queen Kit sat in her seat.

She sat with her chin on her hand.

Queen Kit did not smile.

It was hard to rule the land.

The queen was not mean.

The queen was just glum.

"What can we do to make Queen Kit smile?" her subjects asked each other.

"Maybe a cute dress that is easy to press will please Queen Kit!" said Ned, the dressmaker.

"Maybe a purring pet that is nice and quiet will please Queen Kit!" said Pete, the pet seller. 88 96

"Maybe a flying kite that is shiny and bright will please Queen Kit!" said Tom, the toy maker. 106 114

"Maybe a tasty bite to eat that is not too sweet will please Queen Kit!" said Conrad, the cook. 125 133

"We will surprise the Queen!" said the men. 141

So they hid the cute dress, the purring pet, the flying kite, and the tasty bite to eat. 151 159

Surprise! 160

"Surprise!" said Ned, the dressmaker. "The cut of this cute dress will make you feel better." 167 176

But Ned tripped on the dress and fell, letting out a little yell. 185 189

"Surprise!" said Pete. "This purring pet is perfect!" 195 197

But Pete dropped the pet.   202

And the pet ran away.   207

Pete was so upset.   211

"Surprise!" said Tom. "This flying kite is just   219
right, Queen Kit!"   222

But Tom let it go.   227

And the kite got away.   232

Tom didn't know what to say.   238

"Surprise!" said Conrad. "This tasty bite will be   246
a treat to eat!"   250

But Conrad tripped on his own two feet. And   259
the tasty bite spilled.   263

It spilled on Queen Kit who looked surprised.   271

And what do you think Queen Kit did?   279

Queen Kit smiled.   282

Summer Pen Pals

by Dennis Andersen

illustrated by Meryl Henderson

It's Fun Here

Dear Tammy,

It's fun here at our camp in the forest.
There is so much more to do here than there is
at home.
Yesterday, I waded in the lake.
It's rocky, but I like it.

Jan

Dear Jan,

I know what you mean.
There is always something fun to do.
Here at the beach we go swimming each day.
We have races to see who is the fastest
swimmer.
I am the fastest swimmer in my family.

Tammy

Hi, Tammy!

Last night we hiked in the dark.
The moon looked so big.
A bat flapped near us.
Tim yelled, but I did not!

Jan

Hi, Jan! 120

We all like to go fishing on the dock. 129
Dad always catches the littlest fish. 135
I catch the biggest! 139

              Tammy 140

Tammy, 141

The kids here are really nice. 147
We play games and go for hikes. 154
They all go camping a lot, so they teach me cool 165
things. 166

              Jan 167

Jan, 168

The kids here are nice, too. 174
We make things in the sand and tell stories. 183
They are the funniest! 187

              Tammy 188

It's Not So Much Fun Here 194
Dear Tammy, 196

Mom and I rowed on the lake. 203
It was really windy, and it got cooler and cooler. 213
I still haven't warmed up. 218
Brrr! 219

              Jan 220

Dear Jan,   222

    It's not like that here.   227
    Today is the hottest day since we got here.   236
    I got burned, and it really hurts!   243
    Now I have to stay inside until I am better.   253

          Tammy   254

Hi, Tammy.   256

    Hiking is no fun when it's raining.   263
    The path was muddy, and it got muddier.   271
    I got soaked and dirty.   276
    It still hasn't stopped raining.   281

          Jan   282

Hi, Jan.   284

    We went fishing on a big boat today.   292
    Mom and Dad both got sick, but I got even   302
sicker.   303
    I don't think I like boats very much.   311

          Tammy   312

Dear Tammy,   314

    Can you believe it is still rainy here?   322
    I am tired of everything being wetter than wet. 331
    I can't wait to go home.   337

          Jan   338

Dear Jan, 340

Each day here is warmer than the last. 348
I am tired of everything being hotter than hot. 357
I hope we go home soon, too. 364

Tammy 365

"It's good to be home. I like it much better than 376
camping." 377
"It's much better than the beach, too." 384

Dead as a Dodo, Bald as an Eagle

by Ellen Garin

illustrated by Pat Lucas-Morris

Dead as a Dodo

The stories of the dodo and the bald eagle begin in the same way but have very different endings—one sad and one happy. Read on to see how the story of one bird showed us ways to help the other.

Do you know this saying: "Dead as a dodo"? Do you know what it means?

The dodo was a bird that once lived, but is now extinct. *Extinct* means that there are no more. They have all died.

The dodo was about the size of a turkey. It had a large hooked beak, small wings, and a heavy body with fat yellow legs. The dodo was a bird, but it was unable to fly. It lived in forests on an island in the Indian Ocean.

The story of how the dodo became extinct starts on an island near Africa. It is a place with rich soil and lush plants. 153 164 169

When Dutch settlers landed on the island in 1598, there were many dodoes living there. 177 184

By 1681, less than one hundred years after Dutch settlers first landed, every dodo had died. 192 200

Dodoes built nests on the land but not in trees. When settlers came, they had dogs and wild pigs with them. Pigs and dogs raided dodo nests and ate the eggs. Dodoes laid only one egg at a time, so their eggs were quickly eaten. 210 219 228 240 245

Settlers cleared land for homes and farms. This left dodoes less room for nesting. Dodoes started dying, and before long they had vanished. That is why we say "Dead as a dodo." It means vanished, or extinct. 253 261 270 280 282

Bald as an Eagle 286

Have you ever seen pictures of bald eagles? Most likely, you have. The bald eagle has been the United States's bird since 1782. Its picture is on dollar bills we use every day. 294 304 313 319

The bald eagle has a brown body with a white 329
head and tail. Its beak, eyes, and feet are yellow. 339
Perhaps you know the saying "Bald as an eagle." 348
The bald eagle is not really bald. It got its name 359
from its white head. Unlike dodoes, bald eagles 367
are strong fliers and lay eggs in trees or on high 378
cliffs. Bald eagles live only in North America. 386

In the 1940s, farmers began using a new spray 395
to help get rid of bugs that ruin crops. This spray 406
hurt bald eagles as well as other birds and animals. 416
After being near this spray, many bald eagles could 425
not lay eggs. Those that could, laid eggs with thin 435
shells that cracked before the chicks were ready 443
to hatch. Bald eagles were in trouble. 450

More than bug spray harmed bald eagles. Many 458
eagles lost nests when people cleared land for 466
homes and factories. Eagles had fewer places to 474
live. Just like dodoes, bald eagles began dying. 482

Bald eagles were in trouble, just like dodoes 490
had been. But this time, Americans decided to 498
help. Laws were passed that protected eagle 505
nesting lands. In 1972, the United States stopped 513
using bug spray that hurt eagles. 519

That help came just in time for eagles. There 528
are still not as many bald eagles as before, but 538
things are better. We are learning to care for bald 548
eagles as well as other animals. We are learning to 558
share Earth. 560

Unlike dodoes, bald eagles did not become 567
extinct. Perhaps we learned from the dodo. 574
Perhaps in its own way the dodo saved the bald 584
eagle. 585

Loop and Hook a Dream

by Phillip Ward

illustrated by Pat Lucas-Morris

Granddad Scott Tells Good Tales

The teacher took the children on a field trip to
see Granddad Scott, the storyteller. The children
sat on the wood floor. Granddad Scott stood in
front of the children as he began to tell his colorful
tales of dreams and dreamcatchers.

"When I was a boy, I knew a man named
Running Brook. He made dreamcatchers by
weaving yarn on hoops. I liked sitting with him
while he worked because he told tales of his
dreams."

From a nook in the wall, Granddad took down a
strange-looking thing.

"Running Brook made this dreamcatcher for me 113
out of string, beads, and feathers. He always made 122
something special to share." 126

Granddad Scott shook his dreamcatcher high in 133
the air. He pointed out that the dreamcatcher is 142
like a spiderweb. It is a perfect circle with a hole 153
in the center. 156

"Running Brook told me the bad dreams get 164
caught and tangled in the web part of the 173
dreamcatcher. The good dreams will go through 180
the hole in the center," said Granddad Scott. 188

"Running Brook said that some people hang a 196
dreamcatcher above their beds to sort through the 204
good and bad dreams. The bad dreams are snared 213
in the web. The good dreams slip through the hole 223
and float down the beads and feathers. Only the 232
good dreams land on the dreamer's head to be 241
remembered." 242

Granddad Scott then shared two of his dreams 250
with the children. "In one dream, Hooting Owl 258
says, as he swoops to his tree, 'Be brave and not a 270
fool. Look in books for proof.'" 276

Granddad Scott explained that this dream had a 284
lesson. That is why he remembers it. 291

The second dream Granddad Scott told was a 299
silly one. "Goose Skiddoo is in the doorway of her 309
house. She flaps her wings and stoops low. Then 318
she clears her throat and sings, 'Yellow, blue, red, 327
and green! What can it all mean?'" 334

"Mr. Raccoon stops by and says, 'I'd like to 343
share my lunch with you, Goose Skiddoo.' Goose 351
Skiddoo thanks Mr. Raccoon for his good food. 359
Then she calls to Hooting Owl, 'Please have 367
noodles with us at noon.'" 372

The children laughed about this silly dream.   379

Look! A Dreamcatcher!   382

Granddad Scott asked, "Do you want to make a   391
dreamcatcher? You can loop the hoop your very   399
own way."   401

"You can hook the beads and feathers any way   410
you like, too! Just remember to leave a hole in the   421
center."   422

"Wrap your hoop with cloth. You can choose   430
red, yellow, green, blue, or purple string to loop a   440
web. Soon it will look like the spokes on a bicycle   451
wheel."   452

"Tie a feather to the end of a string, then thread   463
the string with beads. Hook the loose string to the   473
loop. You have made a dreamcatcher! Finally, add   481
a loop so you can hang your dreamcatcher."   489

The children looked at their finished   495
dreamcatchers. "Now you have your own   501
dreamcatchers to hang. Next time you visit, you   509
can share your good dreams with me," said   517
Granddad Scott.   519

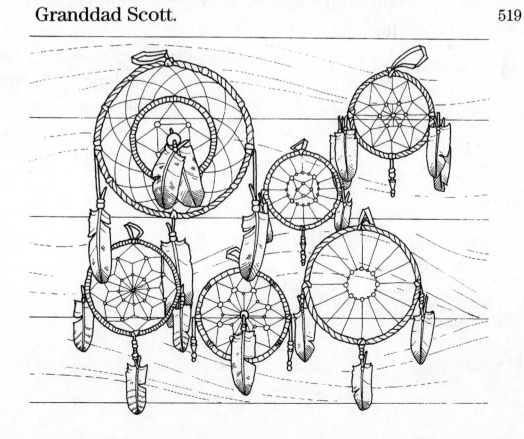

Nesting and Burrowing Birds

by Marilee Robin Burton

illustrated by Meryl Henderson

Nests of All Kinds

There is at least one way that all birds are the same: they lay eggs. To keep the eggs and nestlings safe, most birds make nests. When making nests, however, birds display different skills and styles.

When it is time to make their own nests, most adult birds return to the place where they hatched. Every bird makes the same kind of nest that its parents made.

A lot goes on in nest making. Beaks lift, weave, and drill. Feet stamp and dig! The process may look disorganized, but the nests are very carefully constructed.

We normally think of nests as being in trees. But some birds make nests on rocky cliffs, sandy shores, in the water, and even underground!

Surprisingly, quite a few birds are burrow diggers! They make holes for their nests in trees, logs, cactus plants, and even in the dirt.

4

8

12

16

27

37

45

52

62

71

81

83

92

101

109

111

120

129

136

143

146

149

152

154

157

160

Some birds use the discarded homes of other 168
animals for their nests. They take over the empty 177
den of a rabbit, skunk, or badger. 184

On the following pages you will meet just a few 194
of these fascinating birds. 198

Which Birds Burrow? 201

Bee-Eaters 202

These small, bright birds make holes in 209
riverbanks and cliffs. The common bee-eater 215
repeatedly hurls itself headfirst into the dirt until it 224
makes a dent. Then it stands in the dent and keeps 235
digging to make a deeper tunnel. 241

Burrowing Owls 243

These birds live in treeless grassland. They can 251
dig their own tunnels but prefer to take over 260
someone else's. A prairie dog's deserted home is 268
ideal. If the size is not exactly right, the owl simply 279
enlarges it. It uses its feet to kick dirt backward 289
out of the hole. 293

Elf Owl 295

The elf owl also likes to make its home in 305
deserted holes. A tunnel drilled in a cactus by a 315
woodpecker makes a perfect nest for this tiny owl. 324

Kakapo Parrot 326

The kakapo is the biggest of all parrots. It 335
is a flightless bird and spends its time on the 345
ground. When it is nesting, it looks for holes 354
near tree roots. 357

Crab-Loving Plover   359

The crab-loving plover is the only shorebird that   367
nests underground. These birds live in large flocks   375
and make tunnel homes in sandy spots near the   384
sea. As their name suggests, crab-loving plovers   391
prefer being where crabs are plentiful.   397

Kookaburra   398

The kookaburra, well known for its jungle   405
laugh, nests inside termite homes. It pecks a hole   414
in the termite nest and burrows inside. But the   423
termites don't leave. The bugs build a wall to block   433
the bird's nest.   436

Fairy Prion   438

This bird digs its own home and then gets an   448
uninvited roommate. The tuatara, a prehistoric   454
spiny reptile, shares the nest. During the day, the   463
prion looks for food and the tuatara sleeps. Then   472
at night, the prion returns and the tuatara goes   481
hunting.   482

As you have read, birds provide many styles of   491
homes—from nests to burrows—for their young.   499

Baking Princess

by Barbara Seiger

illustrated by Kersti Frigell

Princess Fay Must Wed

On Sunday, King Raymund went to Princess Fay
and said, "It is time. You must wed. You spend too
much time in this kitchen."

"I have no wish to wed," stated the Princess.
"But if I must, I wish to wed a baker! Then I can
make cakes and tarts with him!"

"It must be a baker who is a prince," added King
Raymund.

"Help Princess Fay!" King Raymund exclaimed.
"She wishes to wed a prince who can bake."

It was in all the papers and on T.V.

"I can bake cakes," said a man named Jake to
his mom, "and my lemon tart is terrific."

"But you are not a prince," said Jake's mom.
"You are fit to dig wells, not to wed a princess and
bake cakes with her."

"But I bake better cakes," said Jake.

"Go mend a fence," said his mom.

"I'd rather make lemon tarts," Jake said.

Jake did not mend the fence as his mom
suggested. He made his best cake, his terrific
lemon tart, and his best muffins. Then he went to
stand with the princes at the gate. They waited and
waited for Princess Fay.

The Contest

"Let's start," said King Raymund to the first
prince.

"My dog Cupcake and I will act as tasters,"
added Princess Fay. "If you can bake cakes and
make tarts, we will wed."

Princess Fay and Cupcake tasted and tasted.

But there was no cake that met Princess Fay's
standards.

"Are things going well?" asked King Raymund.

"Not well at all," said Princess Fay. "Not one of
them can bake cakes or make tarts."

"I can," said Jake. "Just let me have a chance."

"Are you a prince?" asked King Raymund.

"I am not, but just taste," Jake said to Fay, and
handed her his tray.

Princess Fay tasted the tart. "This lemon tart is the best," she said. 322 326

Princess Fay tasted the muffin. "Yum, yum," she said. And then, "Yes, yes, yes! This is the best cake I ever ate." 334 345 348

"But he is not a prince," added King Raymund. 357

"I don't care," said Princess Fay. "The princes did not bake cakes such as this." 365 372

Jake and Princess Fay felt sad. 378

The King felt bad. 382

Then Fay felt glad. 386

"Dad," she said, "I did not wish to wed yet. Let's make Jake the Palace Baker." 397 402

"Yes!" exclaimed King Raymund. "That is the perfect way to fix this problem!" 409 415

Then he turned to Jake, "You will bake with Princess Fay." 424 426

The next day, Jake and Princess Fay made cakes and tarts. 434 437

At the end of the day, Fay gazed at Jake and said to herself, "Perhaps one day. . . ." 448 454

City Girl

by Dennis Andersen

illustrated by Meryl Henderson

"But I can't leave the city, Mommy!" Eve 37
complained. "We have fun here!" 42

Eve's mom tried to make her feel better. "You'll 51
have fun on Steve and Lee's farm, too. You'll see, 61
Sweetie." 62

But it seems her mom did not make Eve feel 72
better at all. Eve still was not sure she wanted to 83
visit the farm. 86

"I'll eat a piece of yummy candy. Then I'll feel 96
better," Eve whispered to herself. 101

But it seems the candy did not make Eve feel 111
better at all. She still was not sure she wanted to 122
visit the farm. 125

Steve and Lee met Eve at the train. 133

"We are very happy you are here!" beamed Steve. 142

"You are a city girl now. But you can be a farm 154
girl, too," added Lee. 158

"I'm happy being a city girl," said Eve. "I am not 169
sure I want to be a farm girl!" 177

"This is our farm," said Steve. 183

"Let's feed these geese," said Steve. 189

Eve peeked at the geese. "I do not like geese," 199
she whispered. 201

"Mom, it's muddy and dirty and dusty here! The   210
geese are mean! Please come and get me. Steve   219
and Lee can come to our home!"   226

"Eve, I can hear that you are tired. I'll pick you   237
up in a week, Sweetie."   242

Letter from Eve

"Here you are! The farm is busy in the day, and
it's busy after dark, too, Eve. Come on and see!"

"What is it?" asked Eve.

"Little bugs," said Lee. "Each bug has a little
beam that twinkles on and off."

"Shhh!" whispered Steve. "See the deer leap?"

"Deer do not leap in the city!" said Eve.

Lee tucked Eve into bed.

"From your bed, you can see the sleepy farm,"
said Steve.

"I'm sleepy, too—like my kitten," Eve said.

"Sweet dreams, farm girl," Lee whispered.

Dear Mom,
   Please do not pick me up in a week.
   The city is pretty, but I like the farm, too.
      Hugs and Kisses,
         Eve

This is my kitten, Fuzzy.

The Frog Who Wanted to Fly

by Barbara Seiger

illustrated by Kersti Frigell

Ivan Can't

Once there was a tiny frog named Ivan. Ivan was not a happy frog. He sighed all the time.

"Why are you sighing?" asked Mr. Pie.

"All my life I've wanted to fly," said Ivan with a sigh.

"Why?" asked Mr. Pie.

"Why not?" said Ivan.

"Frogs can't fly," said Mr. Pie.

"This frog will," Ivan said.

Ivan decided to ask that nice Jane Triangle for help. She was a scientist. She'd tell him how to fly.

While on his way, Ivan heard his name.

"Hello-o-o-o-o! Ivan!" called Pam My-Oh-My. "Can you help me shut this trunk? The top will not shut tightly."

Ivan looked at the trunk. Then he got on top of it and jumped on it with all his might. The trunk shut tightly. "It's fine," he said.

Pam My-Oh-My smiled. "You are very nice. Can I get you mint ice cream?"

"No, thanks," said Ivan, "I'm off to see Jane Triangle. She will tell me how to fly."

"But frogs can't . . ."

"This frog will."

While on his way, Ivan met Sy Bly. "I need to   194
cross the pond," said Sy Bly. "Can you get me to   205
that side?"   207

"Hop on my back," offered Ivan.   213

Sy Bly hopped on.   217

"Now hang on tightly," said Ivan, and jumped   225
into the pond.   228

"Are you all right?" Ivan asked when they had   237
landed.   238

"I'm wet," Sy said. "But I'm fine. Thanks for the   248
ride!"   249

While on his way, Ivan met Dan DeeLight. "Oh,   258
no!" cried Dan DeeLight. "I'm sending cards to ten   267
friends, inviting them to my party. But the tenth   276
stamp is inside this desk. And—just my luck!— the   286
top is stuck. I can't get the stamp!"   294

In no time, Ivan had slipped his long tongue under the top and picked up the stamp. "Here it is," smiled Ivan, the tenth stamp stuck to his tongue.

"Delightful, delightful," exclaimed Dan DeeLight.

Ivan Can

While on his way, Ivan ran right into Jane Triangle herself!

"I was just on my way to see you," said Ivan.

"Well, here I am," said Jane Triangle.

"I want to fly," said Ivan. "You are a scientist. Can you help me?"

"Why do you want to fly?" asked Jane Triangle.

"Who knows?" Ivan said. "But I think about it all the time. It's something I want. A lot," he added.

"Everyone needs something they want a lot," said Jane Triangle. "I wanted to be a scientist all my life. But . . . Ivan, might you be setting your sights too high? You are a *frog*, and frogs can't fly. Frogs do frog things."

"Like?" asked Ivan.

"You can jump," said Pam My-Oh-My. "You are the best jumper I've seen."

"You can swim," said Sy Bly. "You are the best swimmer I've seen."

"And you can grab trapped things with your long tongue," said Dan DeeLight.

"I can't think of anyone who can do all that," said Jane Triangle.

Jane Triangle smiled at Ivan, but Ivan did not smile back. "I can do frog things. Where's the fun in that?" he asked.

303
313
322
323
327
328
330
339
341
352
359
369
373
382
392
402
409
419
428
439
443
446
454
459
469
472
480
485
495
498
507
517
521

"I understand," said Jane Triangle.   526

"I want to do something I can't do," he said.   536

Ivan went home. He thought and thought. Then   544
he brightened. He smiled. He danced a jig. He sang   554
a silly song. Then he called his friend at the lab.   565

"I've made up my mind. This is what I want," he   576
said.   577

Jane Triangle kept quiet while Ivan explained.   584

"But what if it's not right for me? I mean, I *am* a   597
frog," said Ivan.   600

"A frog who fights for what he wants!" added   609
Jane Triangle.   611

"Well, I sat there and I thought—perhaps I can't   621
fly, but maybe I can dive."   627

Rose, the Brave

by Lisa Trumbauer

illustrated by Kersti Frigell

Rose Is Not Afraid

Rose was a princess. But she was not an average princess.

Rose boasted that nothing could scare her. She was very brave.

"I am Rose, the brave!" she would say.

But no one ever believed Rose.

"You just sit on a throne all day. You don't have to be brave to do that," they said.

"Fine," said Rose to herself, "I will just show them that I am as brave as I boast. I will row my boat to the far shore of the moat and show that I am very brave."

Rose rowed her boat to the far shore with no problems.

But when she reached the shore, she was still not happy.

"That was not scary at all," she said. "I need to   139
do something really brave."   143

"I know," Rose said to herself, "I will go into the   154
forest and show that I am really brave."   162

So Rose roamed the forest. The birds chirped,   170
and animals ran near her path.   176

"This is not scary," Rose said. "How will I show   186
that I am brave?"   190

Suddenly a voice said, "Hello!"   195

"Who's there?" Rose asked.   199

"I am a doe," came the reply.   206

Rose had never known a speaking doe before.   214
Rose felt frightened, and so she ran.   221

Rose could not run anymore, so she sat on a   231
large stone. She was upset that she had run when   241
the doe spoke.   244

"I was not frightened," she told herself, "I was   253
just shocked. I am Rose, the brave."   260

"Hello, Rose, the brave," said a voice.   267

"Who's there?" Rose asked.   271

"I am a goat," came the reply.   278

Rose had never known a speaking goat before.   286
Rose felt frightened, and so she ran.   293

"This is silly," said Rose to herself. "I am not   303
frightened of a doe and a goat!" Rose struck a   313
bold pose by a toad on a log and said, "I am Rose,   326
the brave."   328

"Hello, Rose," said the toad. "It's nice to meet   337
you. I am Joe, the toad."   343

Rose had never seen a toad speak before. Rose   352
felt frightened, and so she ran.   358

Rose ran and ran.   362

She ran until she hit her toe.   369

"Ouch," cried Rose, and she fell into a hole.   378
"Oh, no!"   380

Rose Faces Her Fear

"What will I do?" Rose asked herself. 391

"I am not really Rose, the brave. I ran when 401
the doe, the goat, and the toad spoke to me. I 412
was frightened." 414

Rose began to cry. 418

"I am all by myself, stuck in a hole, and I am 430
very frightened." 432

"I must get help," Rose said to herself. "I will 442
wipe my tears and try not to be frightened of the 453
strange animals." 455

"Hello, doe! Hello, goat! Hello, toad!" yelled 462
Rose. "I am stuck in a hole, and I need help." 473

One by one the three animals appeared, and 481
Rose told them how she fell in the hole. 490

"We will help you," said the doe. 497

"Yes, I know just what to do," said the goat. 507

"You don't need to be frightened anymore," 514
added the toad. 517

The doe got a rope, and the goat made a 527
bow. 528

Then the toad let the rope go for Rose to 538
climb up. 540

"Thank you so much," said Rose. "I am sorry I 550
ran when you spoke to me," she added. "I was 560
frightened of you." 563

"It's okay," said the animals. "We are glad we 572
could help. And you don't have to be frightened of 582
us anymore." 584

So Rose left the doe, the goat, and the toad to 595
go home. 597

Rose did not want to admit that she had not 607
acted as bravely as her boast. But she could not 617
delay any longer. The king would be very upset 626
that she went into the forest by herself. 634

The king was angry, but very glad, when Rose 643
got home. 645

"I told you not to go into the forest alone," he 656
scolded Rose. "You are lucky you were not hurt." 665

"I know," said Rose, "but I had to show that I 676
was brave. I will never go into the forest by 686
myself again." 688

Then Rose told the tale of her day. When she 698
got to the end, she said, "I was not so brave after 710
all. In fact, I was very frightened." 717

"Maybe you were frightened, but you were 724
brave as well," said the King. 730

"You faced a fear, and that is very brave. You 740
really are Rose, the brave." 745

Rose smiled and struck her bold pose. 752

Whales

by Barbara Seiger

illustrated by Meryl Henderson

Types of Whales

Whales may spend most of their time
underwater, but they are quite different from fish.
Whales have lungs and smooth skin. Fish breathe
with gills and are covered with scales. Whales
swim differently, too. Both fish and whales use
their tails to swim. But a fish tail goes from side to
side while a whale tail goes up and down.

Like humans, whales are mammals. Baby
whales do not hatch out of eggs like fish. Baby
whales grow inside the mother and are alive
during birth. After its birth, the baby stays close to
its mother so it can reach her milk quickly.

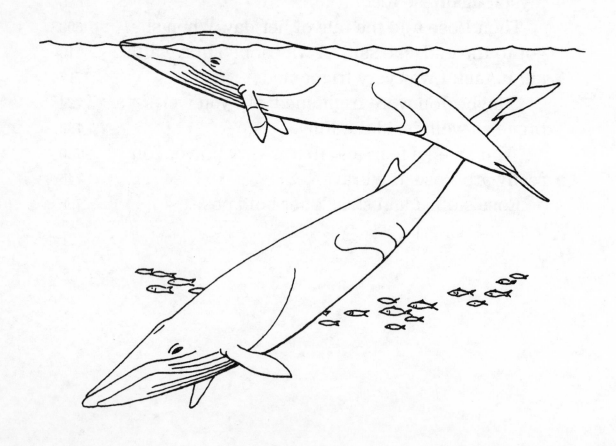

Like other mammals, whales need air. A whale 122
cannot breathe in liquid, so it must swim to the top 133
of the water to get air. Before it goes back under, a 145
whale will fill up its lungs just like we do before we 157
dive. Some whales need fresh air frequently. They 165
swim up every two to three minutes. Others, like 174
the piked whale, can stay under for 120 minutes. 183

During birth, a baby whale doesn't breathe. As 191
soon as it is born, the baby must swim up and fill 203
its lungs with air. If a new baby has difficulty 213
swimming, the mother will help. 218

When a whale is underwater, air in its lungs gets 228
hot and damp. When a whale needs fresh air, it 238
rises up and blows the old air out of a blowhole on 250
top of its body. When the hot air hits colder 260
outside air, it turns into fog. 266

There are two different types of whales, based 274
on how they eat. Some whales have teeth. But they 284
do not use these teeth to chew. These 292
whales use their teeth only to catch 299
their meals. 301

The killer whale or orca is one type 309
of whale with teeth. Orcas have 315
very sharp teeth. The name *killer* 321
whale makes orcas seem scary. 326
But don't be frightened. An 331
orca will not go after humans. 337
It uses its sharp teeth only 343
on whales and fish. 347

Baleen whales have no teeth. In place of teeth, they have baleen plates. When the whale feeds, it takes in a lot of water. Then, when it pushes the water back out, the baleen acts as a strainer. Tiny fish that were in the water are left behind for the whale to eat.

Biggest Whale

Blue whales are huge. In fact, they are bigger than any other creature. A blue whale can be more than 100 feet long, but most are 70–90 feet. This is longer than four buses placed end to end. Blue whales can weigh up to 150 tons. Lifting a blue whale would be like picking up more than thirty elephants.

As huge as it is, the blue whale can still jump up out of the water, and swim on its back. It's quick, too, swimming up to twenty miles per hour. Its strong tail helps the blue whale swim fast and jump high.

Blue whales must eat a lot. They eat mainly krill, a shrimp like creature. Each whale must consume one to two tons of krill each day.

356
365
376
386
397
400
402
411
420
431
441
451
460
462
474
485
494
502
505
511
516
519
522
526
529
531

Experts think that blue whales communicate 537
with hums. Adult whales hum in deep, cold water. 546
The cold helps the hums travel better. These hums 555
can travel as far as 100 miles. When humans hear 565
these hums, it seems that whales are singing 573
pretty songs. 575

At one time blue whales thrived. Whalers 582
hunted blue whales for their meat and whale oil. 591
Hunting reached its peak in 1931, and by 1966 600
there were so few blue whales left that a ban was 611
placed on hunting them. 615

Today, fewer than 10,000 blue whales survive. 622
For every blue whale alive today, there used to 631
be twenty. Blue whales continue to be protected. 639
You can see them off the California coast in 648
late summer. 650

Using Your Cents

by David Grahm

It was Cindy's birthday, and as usual, her
grandparents gave her some birthday money.

"Buy yourself something special," they told her.

Cindy never had trouble deciding how to spend
the money. She always went to Al's Toy Store, a
store with a large selection of toys. She would
look over Al's collection of stuffed animals. It
included bears, monkeys, sheep, birds, fish, and
more. Some were big, and some were babies. Each
year, Cindy would buy the one or two animals she
liked most.

This year was different, however. Cindy entered
the store and looked at the shelves, but she could
not find any animals she really liked.

At last she thought, "I guess the big red foxes
look okay, and so do the babies." She used her last
pennies to pay for them.

At home, Cindy added the foxes to the rest of   150
her collection, but she played with them very little   159
because she didn't like them that much.   166

Several months later, Cindy was strolling by Al's   174
Toy Store. In the window she saw some new   183
stuffed animals, including baby goats, deer, and   190
mice. She really wanted to have them.   197

"Now, those babies are really cute!" Cindy   204
thought. "But I have no money to pay for them.   214
Maybe I can make a trade."   220

She entered the store and talked to Al.   228

"Sorry, Cindy," Al said, "but you bought the   236
foxes a long time ago. I can't let you trade them   247
now for the newer animals. That wouldn't be fair."   256

Later, Cindy told her parents her problem.   263

"Let this be a lesson," her father said. "When   272
you have money, you don't have to spend it all   282
right away. Save it until you are sure of what you   293
want to buy. That makes good cents!"   300

The Hare and the Tortoise

retold by Linda Kries

	5
	9

Hare and Tortoise were friends. One day 16
Tortoise said, "Let's have a race. That will be fun." 26

"It may be fun," Hare laughed, "but you can't 35
win. You are much too slow, Tortoise." 42

"We shall see," Tortoise said, smiling. 48

The two friends started to race around the lake. 57
Hare hopped very quickly, while Tortoise crawled 64
very slowly. 66

Soon Hare was far ahead of Tortoise. 73

"I am so far in front," Hare thought. "I'll stop 83
and rest here a while before finishing the race." 92

Hare stopped to rest. Soon she was fast asleep 101
even though she hadn't planned on doing that. 109

Meanwhile, Tortoise kept on crawling. He went   116
slowly but moved along, little by little. He never   125
stopped.   126

In time, Tortoise had caught up with Hare. Hare   135
was still sleeping soundly. Tortoise quietly crawled   142
past without waking her up.   147

Tortoise was almost around the whole lake. Just   155
then, Hare woke up. She saw Tortoise far ahead.   164
She hopped fast to beat him, but it was too late.   175
Tortoise had won the race!   180

What can you learn from this tale? Slow and   189
steady wins the race! So don't fall asleep on   198
the job.   200

Where Did That Dollar Bill Come From?

by Stephen Howard

A long time ago, there was no such thing as a 21
dollar bill. Can you believe that there was no need 31
for it? Can you imagine living without money? It is 41
hard to believe now, but that is how it used to be. 53
Here is how the dollar bill came to be. 62

Trading vs. the Dollar Bill 67

Before there was money, people used to trade, 75
or barter, goods and services. People traded things 83
such as shells, corn, tobacco, and animals. People 91
traded these things for the food and clothing they 100
needed or wanted. 103

When the European settlers, or colonists, came 110
to North America, they soon began using the 118
Spanish "pieces of eight." These were silver coins 126
known as "dollars." Eventually, 12 of the 13 134
colonies of settlers, or the Continental Congress, 141
issued their own coins and paper 147
money called 149
"bills." Coins and 152
bills were made 155
the official 157
currency, or money, 160
of the land. Thus, 164
the first dollar 167
bill of the 170
United States 172
was born. 174

Printing the Dollar Bill

The earliest United States dollars were printed on regular paper. Today, bills are printed on a special blend of 25% cotton and 75% linen. This special blend makes a dollar bill stronger and last longer. No one can make this special blend without the United States Bureau of Engraving and Printing saying they can. People can't just make their own money. All money of the United States is very carefully made. The same kinds of coins or bills are exactly the same in size, weight, and the way they look. That is so nobody gets confused.

Every country in the world has its own money. But, the money of the United States is the most widely used money in the world today.

The Good-Luck Pen

by Jake Marks

3

6

Brad loved to write silly stories. Once he wrote
about a cook's son who always made dinner for
breakfast. Another story was about Red Riding
Hood's baby brother, Robin Hood! And once he
wrote about a neighbor's tree that danced on a
wood foot!

Friends often asked Brad how he got his ideas.
Brad would say, "I have a good-luck pen. That's
how I write my stories."

Every day, Brad imagined the strangest people,
places, and things. He took notes on his ideas in a
book. Later, he used the notes to make up his
stories. And, of course, he always used his good-
luck pen.

One day, Brad wanted to write a new story.
But he could not find
his good-luck pen
anywhere. He
looked in his book,
his backpack, and
his pocket. He
looked high and
low. But Brad's good-
luck pen was nowhere
to be found!

15
24
31
39
48
50
59
68
73
80
91
101
110
111
120
125
128
130
134
137
140
143
147
150
153

Brad didn't know what to do. In school, his   162
friends saw his usual smile was missing.   169

"What's wrong?" they asked.   173

"I can't find my good-luck pen," Brad explained. 181
"Without my good-luck pen, I can't write my silly 190
stories."   191

"That's all right," Trisha said. "You can use my 200
pen instead."   202

"But it's not my good-luck pen," Brad cried. "I   211
don't think I can write without it."   218

Trisha said, "Brad, you don't need a good-luck   226
pen to write with. You can write a good story with 237
any pen."   239

"I'll try," Brad said.   243

That day, Brad wrote a story about a cookie that 253
swam in a brook. It was the silliest story ever! And 264
Brad had learned something important.   269

"I don't need a good-luck pen to write good   278
stories," he said. "I just need a good imagination, 287
and I always have that with me."   294

Airport Weekends

by Pamela J. Lee-Green

Every weekend, Tim goes with his mother to the airport. That's where she works at a part-time job. Tim keeps busy while his mother works.

Tim is adventurous when he visits the airport. Sometimes he explores the different stores. Sometimes he watches the airplanes take off and land. A few times he has seen famous people. Most often he talks to the different people coming and going.

Tim loves taking pictures. He always takes his camera with him to the airport.

Many people who are happy to be returning   95
home to their families ask Tim to take their   104
pictures. Then they pay him three to five dollars   113
for the pictures. Tim is always courteous and   121
thanks them. He saves the money he earns.   129

One Saturday morning, Tim has an idea. Tim   137
asks his mother how much money she earns   145
working at the airport each weekend. His mother   153
tells him she makes $112 for two days. He   162
disappears into his room to count his money. Tim   171
has $72. He needs to do more work.   179

Tim takes more photos. Soon he has enough   187
money. He talks to his mother again about her job   197
at the airport. This time Tim gives his mother $112   207
that he has saved. He asks his mother to take a   218
weekend off so they can do something fun   226
together. Tim's mother smiles. She agrees they   233
need a fun weekend away from the airport.   241

Little Bear's Trick

by Gretchen Weller

3

6

In the forest, many of the animals were friends.   15
Every day you could find Snake, Woodpecker,   22
Elephant, Peacock, and Little Bear together. They   29
were always laughing, talking, and playing.   35

Sometimes, the animals would show each other   42
tricks they could do. One morning, Woodpecker   49
sat on a tree and began to peck with her beak.   60
Soon, she had made a large hole in the tree.   70

"I would certainly like to do that," Little Bear   79
said. He pecked his nose against the tree. But it   89
only made his nose hurt!   94

After that, Snake stretched until his head   101
touched his tail.   104

"I would certainly like to do that," Little Bear   113
said. He stretched as far as he could, but it was   124
hopeless. His head did not reach his tail.   132

Next, Peacock spread his beautiful feathers.   138
They appeared and then disappeared.   143

"I would certainly like to do that," Little Bear 152
said. But he quickly discovered that he had no 161
feathers to spread, so he couldn't do that. 169

Lastly, Elephant lifted a leafy tree right out of 178
the ground to show how strong he was. 186

"I would certainly like to do that," Little Bear 195
said. He took hold of a tree and pulled and pulled 206
again. But the tree stayed unmoved. 212

Little Bear sat on the ground, filled with 220
sadness. He wanted a trick to show his friends, 229
too. But what might that be? 235

Suddenly Little Bear had an idea. He stood up 244
and went over to Elephant. Little Bear gave her a 254
big hug. Then he did the same to Peacock. Next, 264
he gave a hug to Woodpecker. And finally, he gave 274
a hug to Snake. 278

"Now I know what my trick is!" Little Bear 287
cried. "I can give bear hugs each day to all 297
my friends!" 299

And so he did! 303

Two Goats and a Sheep, Please!

by Susan Hand

You may think that money always has been like   18
the coins that you use to buy a newspaper. Or you   29
may think of it as the paper bills that your parents   40
use to buy some food or clothes. But many, many   50
years ago people did not have coins or bills. So   60
they found other interesting ways to pay for what   69
they wanted.   71

Trading Animals   73

The first kind of money was animals on people's   82
farms. Over 8,000 years ago, people traded cattle   90
for whatever else they needed. One neighbor might   98
give a goat, a sheep, or a cow. Then, the other   109
neighbor might give that person some clothes or   117
food in trade. That may seem strange to us today.   127
But even stranger things were used for money   135
years ago.   137

Money Around the World 141

Over 2,000 years ago, leather was used in China. 150
The piece of leather was made in the shape of a 161
square. Each side was one foot long. It was made 171
from deerskin and had borders of many colors. 179
It was like the paper money we have today, 188
only bigger. 190

Here in America, as far back as 1535 or even 200
before, Native Americans used strings or belts of 208
beads as money. Some strings were over six feet 217
long. The beads were mainly made from clam 225
shells. This bead money was called "wampum." 232
Wampum means "white," the color of some shells. 240

Long ago, people in Greece used tiny apple 248
seeds for money. The people who got the seeds 257
could use them to plant their own trees. 265

Money Today 267

Money changes all the time, even to this day. A 277
few years ago, the United States decided to change 286
the $100 bill. Like the old $100 bill, the new one 297
has a picture of Ben Franklin on its face. But now, 308
his picture and some letters on the front and back 318
of the bill are bigger. 323

Some people say that paper money will not be 332
around 50 or 150 years from now. They say we will 343
pay for things only on the computer. 350

The New Picasso

by Susan Shafer

3

6

When you paint a picture, you might feel so
proud you want to hang it on your refrigerator.
When Alexandra Nechita paints a picture, it might
hang in a museum. That's because Alexandra has
been a world-famous painter since she was about
ten years old. Her paintings are shown in some of
the largest museums in the world. They sell for
thousands of dollars. Her style is her own. But
many people compare her work to paintings by a
famous artist named Picasso.

A World of Color

Picasso was the best-known artist of the
last 100 years. He also started to paint
when he was about ten years old. He
lived to the age of 91, making works of
art right to the end. During his
whole life he made about 20,000
works of art.

Like Picasso, Alexandra uses
bright colors. And like Picasso,
she does not always paint
things the way they really look.
She paints things as she imagines
them. That's what makes
her succeed. She
loves to paint so
much she would do it
even if she could not sell
her work.

15
24
32
40
48
58
67
76
85
89
93
101
109
117
126
133
139
142
146
151
156
162
168
172
175
179
184
190
192

Coloring Books at Age Two

Alexandra started with coloring books when
she was little. She was only two years old. Now
she has a whole room in her house for her
painting. She paints about three hours a day. She
has lots of friends. Alexandra was not born in this
country. She was born in a country called
Romania, which is in Europe. She came to
America when she was two years old.

Now a teenager, Alexandra goes to school and
takes classes like any other schoolgirl. She did not
take her first art class in school until she was
about 11, after she was already a famous painter.

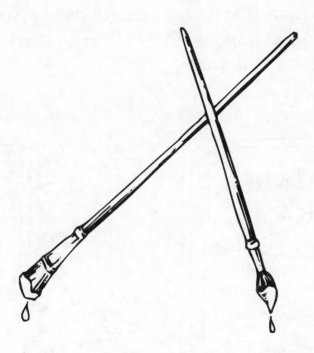

197
203
213
223
232
242
250
258
265
273
282
292
301

A Valuable Lesson

by Sarah Carver

It was a bright and sunny afternoon. Manny had   15
just left dance class with his father and was on his   26
way home. He walked with a bouncy step, still   35
thinking about the new dance he'd just learned.   43

Every lesson he took was memorable, but   50
today's lesson had seemed really special. His   57
teacher had taught him some quick, jumpy moves,   65
like dancing on air! What a valuable lesson it   74
had been!   76

On the street, Manny came to a shady spot   85
under a large tree. Looking down at his feet, he   95
caught sight of something on the grass. He looked   104
closer and saw that it was money! Manny stopped,   113
picked it up, and unfolded it. It was a crisp five-   124
dollar bill—unbelievable!   126

3
6

FIRST NATIONAL BANK

COMMUNITY PLAY CENTER DONATIONS

Manny looked around to see if anyone had just 135
dropped it. No one else was around. 142

"Guess it's my lucky day," Manny said, putting 150
the bill in his pocket. 155

As he continued walking, Manny looked into 162
store windows. He began to think how he might 171
spend the money. He could buy a yo-yo, he 180
thought. Or, he might save it until he had enough 190
for a small portable radio. 195

"I don't want to make any quick decisions," he 204
thought. 205

Just then, Manny saw a sign in a bank window 215
asking for donations for a new play center. It said 225
that the center would have special play areas with 234
exciting things for children in the town. It said 243
there would be classes in art, dance, cooking, 251
sports, and much more for everyone. Manny 258
thought this sounded like something that would do 266
a lot of good for a lot of people. It certainly was a 279
worthwhile project. He decided to donate his 286
money. Manny and his dad went inside the bank. 295
The teller smiled at Manny and showed him where 304
to put the money. 308

Manny smiled back at her, feeling even better 316
than before. He had helped a worthy cause on 325
his own. 327

"Another valuable lesson," he said, dancing on 334
air the rest of the way home with a new bounce in 346
his step. 348

Max and the Watchtower

by Margaret Young

There was nothing special about Max's town, 14
except for the old fire watchtower in the middle of 24
the fields near his house. No one went there to 34
watch for fires anymore. But Max went there every 43
day. That's where he went to lead his crew! 52

All around the tower were fields of soybeans as 61
far as the eye could see. Every day after school, 71
Max hurried home, did his homework, and raced 79
to the tower. 82

Max would climb the tower steps. On the tower, 91
he was no longer a boy. He became Captain Max, 101
sailing his trusty boat called *Royal Blue*. He and 110
his crew were looking for a sunken treasure of 119
gold coins. 121

Max would look out across the sea and then 130
study his map for the location of the gold. Then he 141
would point his spyglass at the fields, raise his 150
voice, and steer his crew to riches. They would toil 160
long and hard for their captain. They were loyal to 170
him. This gave Captain Max great joy. 177

It was almost dark when Max returned home to 186
join his parents for dinner. They always knew 194
where he had been. Every day they asked him the 204
same questions. 206

"What did you do at that old tower today?" 215
asked his mother. 218

"Anything new out there?" asked his father. 225

Max always smiled and replied, "Same old sea 233
of plants as far as the eye can see." But they knew 245
he always saw much more! 250

The Money Tree

by Wendy Williams

When I was nine years old, I wanted to buy everything under the sun. I had no money to buy it with, but that didn't stop me from asking.

Whenever Mom and I walked by a toy store, I looked in the window. There were roller skates, teddy bears, and baseballs.

"Mom, Mom, I want that! I want that!" I would shout. Mom always just smiled and shook her head no.

"Sorry, son, but money doesn't grow on trees, you know," she would say.

When I walked through town with Dad, we would go past a game room. Kids inside were playing all kinds of games.

"Dad, Dad, let's play!" I would shout. Dad always smiled and shook his head no.

"Sorry, son, but money doesn't grow on trees, you know," he would say.

But one day, I proved that it does.

My sister and I were outdoors, playing our 156
favorite board game. We were sitting at a table 165
under a large oak tree. 170

Suddenly, a strong wind came along and blew 178
right across our game. Part of the game was a box 189
of play money. All the money flew high into the air. 200
I thought it was gone forever, but then an amazing 210
thing happened. The money blew into the tree and 219
stayed in its branches! Can you imagine? Hundreds 227
of bills were hanging from that tree! 234

I ran indoors, got our camera, and snapped a 243
photo of the tree. I sent it to the newspaper with 254
this caption: "Money does grow on trees!" The 262
newspaper liked the picture and printed it. They 270
even paid me ten dollars—real dollars! 277

Now, whenever my parents say, "Money doesn't 284
grow on trees," I show them the photo. I laugh and 295
say, "Oh, yes, it does!" 300

Hansel and Gretel

retold by Liz Bravo

Once there lived a very poor man. He had two   17
small children. The boy was named Hansel, and   25
the girl was named Gretel. The family had very   34
little, but they were all very happy.   41

One day, there was almost no food in the house.   51
So Hansel and Gretel left their home. The children   60
began to walk far into the woods to find food.   70

"How will we find our way back home?" Hansel   79
asked Gretel.   81

"We will drop bits of bread as we walk," Gretel   91
explained. "That way, we can follow them back to   100
the house later."   103

Soon the two children saw a beautiful house   111
made of gingerbread. Hansel broke off a piece of   120
the roof to eat.   124

A woman inside heard the noise.   130

"Come in!" she called pleasantly. The woman   137
then tried to push Gretel into a cooking pot! But   147
Hansel and Gretel ran away quickly.   153

The two children looked to find the bits of   162
bread. But they were gone! Birds had eaten the   171
crumbs. They thought that they were lost.   178

Luckily, their father found them. The children   185
told their father what had happened.   191

"I am so happy you are safe!" he cried.   200

The Fable of the Greedy Little Woman

retold by Daniel Bland

4
7
11

Once there was a greedy little woman who owned a hen. The greedy little woman was quite pleased with the hen. "Yes, indeed, what a lovely hen I have!" she said to herself. "Those other hens hardly lay once in a while. Mine never misses a single day."

19
28
37
47
57
59

One day, the greedy little woman started to wonder how many eggs she had in her henhouse. She counted three dozen. "I will take them to town and sell them before a thief takes them from me," she said. And off the greedy little woman went to town, clutching her basket full of eggs.

67
76
86
96
106
113

It was a long way to town, and the greedy little woman was lonely. After a brief while, she started to think to make the time go by more quickly. "How much will I be able to get for my eggs?" she thought. "What shall I do for myself when I receive all that money?"

124
133
143
155
160
165
168

As the greedy little woman walked, she began spending all the money in her mind. She will buy six hens that will each lay an egg a day. She will sell half of the eggs and let the rest hatch. Soon she will have a henhouse full of chickens and eggs. "Oh, good for me, I will be rich, indeed!" she said with a greedy giggle.

172
176
181
187
193
199
205
210
215
220
226
230
234

"I'll be a fancy lady," the greedy little woman
said to herself. "I'll be so fine and proud I can turn
up my nose at everyone and everything." As the
eggs heard her say that, they leaped from the
basket and hit the ground. CRASH! CRACK!
SPLAT! SPLATTER!

"Oh, good grief, indeed!" the greedy little
woman cried. "It doesn't pay to count your
chickens before they hatch."

The Fortune Brothers

by Melissa Redman

3

6

15
23
32
40
46
56
66
68
76
85
94
103
109
119
124
133
139
148
158
167
176
185
189

Once upon a time there were two brothers. The rich and greedy brother was called Good Fortune. The poor but generous one was called Ill Fortune. Good Fortune loved gold more than anything. Ill Fortune loved giving more than anything.

One day, Good Fortune was hiding his gold in a cave, as he did every day. Suddenly he saw a golden light.

The glowing figure said, "Good Fortune, with all of your riches, and your brother so poor, surely you will share your wealth with your brother and have good luck for the rest of your days."

"Never!" shouted Good Fortune. He kept counting his gold. "This is my gold, and I shall share it with no one!"

"This is very bad," said the glowing figure. "You will be sorry." Then it disappeared.

The next day Good Fortune woke up early. He went to count his gold, as he did every morning. When he finished counting, he realized he had only half of the gold he had yesterday. Good Fortune became very upset. He vowed to punish the person who took his gold.

The morning after that, Good Fortune went to   197
count his gold. All of the gold was gone! He ran   208
home sobbing and screaming. As he was running,   216
Good Fortune met his brother Ill Fortune on   224
the road.   226

Happily, Ill Fortune told his brother of the good   235
luck that had come to him. He had been plowing in   246
the field when he hit upon a pot of gold. Sadly,   257
Good Fortune told his brother of his misfortune.   265
Now, the poor brother was rich and the rich   274
brother was poor.   277

Ill Fortune gladly shared his good fortune with   285
his brother. They both lived forever more, sharing   293
their fortunes with one another and others.   300

How Tigers Got Their Stripes

A folktale from Thailand

Retold by Jeri Cipriano

Long ago in Thailand, tigers did not have black stripes on their coats. They had fur as golden as the sun.

But Thailand had rainy seasons. The rain came down hard and caused floods. People got ready. They stored food. They built their houses on tall posts to keep them high above water.

One day a basket maker went into the forest to cut some palm stems. He needed the long thin stems of palm trees to make his baskets. In the forest, he met a golden tiger. The tiger looked angry.

The basket maker was afraid. "If you eat me, you will not live long," he told the tiger. He explained that the heavy rains would flood the forest. The animals would not be safe.

"Let's be good neighbors," the man said. "If you   148
let me go, I will make you a raft," he said. "I will   161
tie you to the raft. You will float and not drown."   172

"But I weigh too much," the tiger said, smiling.   181
"Besides, I'm not a mouse. I don't need a raft. I can   193
climb a tree to stay out of the water."   202

"The floods will last a long time," the basket   211
maker said. "There will be strong gusts of wind.   220
Many trees will fall. You may die if you don't have   231
a raft."   233

The tiger began to worry. Finally, he agreed to   242
let the man make him a raft. The basket maker   252
made a raft quickly. He tied the tiger to it with   263
ropes. Then he hurried home.   268

That night, the sky grew dark, but it did not   278
rain. The next night it did not rain either. The tiger   289
was furious. The basket maker had tricked him!   297
The more he thought about it, the more enraged   306
the tiger became. He twisted to free himself from   315
the ropes. Each time he twisted, the ropes left   324
dark marks on his coat. After eight tries, the tiger   334
was free. So from that day on, tigers have had dark   345
stripes on their golden coats.   350

Why Corn Is Yellow

A Folktale from Mexico

retold by Linda Ward Beech

4

8

13

Long ago in Mexico, corn was not yellow. It was blue.

Back then, there was a farmer named Eduardo. He loved the sun. Each morning he raced to see it rise. He watched its golden glow. He felt its soft heat.

Eduardo watched the sun climb up to the clouds. He saw the sun wake the flowers. He saw it shine down on his fields of blue corn.

All day, Eduardo watched the sun. He watched it as he worked. He watched it when he leaned on his hoe and rested.

At night, Eduardo watched the sun set. "Where does it go?" he wondered. "I must find out."

22
24
32
42
52
54
62
72
81
89
100
104
112
121

One day, Eduardo followed the sun. He walked 129
and walked. At last he came to the sea. There he 140
saw the sun tell the sky good night. Then, the 150
sun sank into the sea. As it did, a gold flame lit 162
the water. 164

"So this is where the sun goes," said Eduardo. 173
"Each night it gives the sea a blanket of gold." 183

Eduardo thought about the sun's gold. How fine 191
it would be to have some for himself. "I will take 202
just a little," he said. 207

He dipped some pails into the sea. He filled 216
them with the gold that the sun had left there. 226

Then, Eduardo started for home. He walked and 234
walked. At last he was close to his farm. He had 245
only one more hill to climb. Up, up he went in the 257
black night. 259

But just as he reached the top, Eduardo fell! 268
The pails tumbled down the hill. And the gold 277
flowed over Eduardo's field. 281

"Oh, no!" cried Eduardo. "I have lost the gold! 290
That's what I get for taking it." 297

Eduardo was sad. But he had learned a lesson. 306
He went back to tending his fields. 313

Soon the corn was ripe. It was time for Eduardo 323
to pick it. What a surprise he had! His corn was no 335
longer blue. It was yellow! 340

Eduardo smiled when he saw the corn. He 348
remembered the pails of gold that he had spilled. 357
And that is how corn became yellow like the sun. 367

Hello, Hans Christian Andersen

by Susan Elliot

1

4

7

15

23

31

38

46

56

64

75

85

93

102

104

108

117

126

135

143

151

160

169

178

185

194

203

212

216

Do you know the story "The Emperor's New Clothes"? Or "The Snow Queen"? Or "The Ugly Duckling"? All of these great stories and dozens more were written by the same man.

His name was Hans Christian Andersen. He was born almost 200 years ago in a little town in Denmark. His father was a gentle shoemaker who did not make a lot of money. But Hans's father did make puppets and read stories to Hans to pass the time away. Young Hans proudly learned how to work the puppets and would make up little stories for them.

From Duckling to Swan

In school Hans was not liked by the other children. They made fun of him because he was thin and not very handsome. But Hans felt that even though others thought he was an "ugly duckling," inside he was really a beautiful swan.

Hans's father died when Hans was 11. A few years later Hans decided to become a writer. But he did not write children's stories. He wrote plays, poetry, long books, and especially, travel books.

Hans loved to travel. For years he would travel all over Europe and write about what he saw. Before he ever wrote one children's story, he was already a famous writer.

The Master of the Fairy Tale

One day Hans decided to write down some of
the stories he heard during his travels. The stories
became popular, especially with children. Hans
was surprised because he had written them for
adults. Even today, children all over the world love
"Thumbelina" and "The Red Shoes."

Hans didn't make up most of the first stories he
wrote. They were old stories called fairy tales or
folktales. They are stories about friendly giants
and scary dragons. Everyone liked them so much,
Hans later decided to write some of his own.
These turned out to be some of his best stories.
You really can't tell the difference between the real
fairy tales and the ones that Hans made up.

All in all, Hans wrote almost 190 stories.

Nellie Bly, Star Reporter

by John Savage

Nellie Bly was born in 1867. When she was in her teens, she decided she would be a newspaper reporter. People thought that was silly. It seemed like a wild idea. A girl reporter? In those days? Why, that would never do!

But Nellie had made up her mind. She showed her work to the editor of a newspaper.

He gave her a job—even though she was a girl. And she was only eighteen! Maybe he thought she'd write about gardens.

But Nellie didn't write about gardens. She wrote   97
about how bad things were in the city slums. Once   107
she even pretended to lose her mind. That way she   117
got into an insane asylum. She wrote about what it   127
was like. Soon she was a star reporter.   135

In 1889 Nellie had her big idea. She had read a   146
book called *Around the World in Eighty Days*.   154
She was sure that she could beat that. She'd go   164
around the world in less than eighty days!   172

She started out on November 14, 1889. During   180
the trip she traveled by ocean liner, train, and   189
ricksha. She rode horses and burros. Days and   197
weeks went by. People everywhere read about her   205
trip. The paper she worked for started a contest.   214
"Guess how long it will take Nellie to go round the   225
world!" A million people made guesses.   231

How long did it take her? Nellie Bly came home   241
to the United States after seventy-two days, six   249
hours, eleven minutes, and fourteen seconds. That   256
trip made her famous all over the world.   264

Nellie Bly died in 1922, but people still   272
remember her.   274

Tall Tales

by David Carver

Stories can be told in many ways. They can be written down. They can be told aloud. They can be shown through pictures. Did you know that sometimes these pictures are carved on trees?

The Native Americans along the Pacific Coast had no written words. So they carved their stories on trees. These trees are called totem poles.

Making a Totem Pole

Here's how they made totem poles. First they cut down a tree. Then artists carved figures all along the trunk of the tree. The artist with the best imagination carved the most important figures. The figures might be animals, like frogs or foxes. Or they might be carvings of the sun and the moon, or the chief or his daughter. Together these carvings told a story.

The Totem Pole Story

The totem pole was like a family album on a tree. It might tell if the family had a lot of money or power. The totem pole could tell about brothers and sisters. It could show aunts and uncles. If an uncle was a good fisherman, the artist might carve a picture of a salmon. If he was brave, you might see the face of a bear.

Finishing the Totem Pole

208

The totem pole was sometimes painted. 214
Then it was lifted so it stood up straight. 223
Some totem poles are still standing after 230
100 years. 232

The most important carvings were 237
usually at the bottom because it was 244
hard to see the tops of the poles. Some 253
totem poles were 60 feet tall or more. 261
That's as high as 12 children standing on 269
each other's shoulders! 272

The next time you see a picture of a 281
totem pole, look at it carefully. Use the 289
carvings to read about the life of a Native 298
American family. 300

How Beaver Got His Home

by Judy Yero

Long ago, Beaver was resting in the woods. He 17
was almost asleep when he heard a loud fluttering 26
in the trees. Beaver looked up and noticed Crow 35
settling onto a branch. 39

"Caw, caw!" called Crow in his usual loud, 47
annoying way. 49

"Oh, no!" thought Beaver. "I'll never get any 57
rest with that noisy Crow up there." So Beaver 66
kicked up some dust and thumped his tail against 75
Crow's tree. 77

Sure enough, Crow was frightened and quickly 84
flew away. 86

Mouse was strolling across the field. When he 94
spied Crow flying out of the trees, Mouse became 103
frightened. He thought Crow would swoop down 110
and catch him. So Mouse began to run very fast. 120

Because Mouse kept looking back over his 127
shoulder, he ran right into a pumpkin vine. A large 137
pumpkin broke loose and rolled down the hill. 145

"Eek!" cried Rabbit as she saw the pumpkin 153
speeding toward her. Rabbit bumped into several 160
logs as she raced to her burrow under the 169
woodpile. 170

One big log started tumbling down the hill. It 179
nearly squashed two baby ducklings eating near 186
the woodpile. 188

Mother Duck was very angry. "Why did you 196
push that log?" she quacked angrily to Rabbit. "You 205
could have hurt my ducklings!" 210

"It wasn't my fault," replied Rabbit. "A big 218
pumpkin was chasing me." 222

"Pumpkin!" shouted Mother Duck. "Why did you 229
chase Rabbit? It's your fault that the log fell." 238

"Oh, no," said Pumpkin. "It was that clumsy 246
Mouse who ran into me and knocked me from 255
my vine." 257

"Mouse!" yelled Mother Duck. "Do you know 264
what you almost did with all your careless 272
running around?" 274

"Not I," said Mouse. "I was just trying to get 284
away from Crow, who was about to eat me." 293

Mother Duck spied Crow on a fence post. 301
"Crow!" she screamed. "You almost got my 308
baby ducklings squashed! Why were you 314
chasing Mouse?" 316

"I wasn't chasing Mouse," cawed Crow. 322
"Something was trying to knock down my tree, 330
so I flew away." 334

Mother Duck wouldn't give up. She found 341
Crow's tree and saw the flattened grass and little 350
paw prints in the dirt. Sure enough, there was 359
Beaver sleeping in his favorite spot. 365

"Beaver! It was all your fault!" she scolded. 373

"What was all my fault?" Beaver asked. 380

Mother Duck's patience had run out. "This is 388
what you get for trying to hurt my ducklings," she 398
cried. Then she snapped angrily at Beaver with 406
her bill. 408

Beaver didn't know why Mother Duck was so 416
mad, but he didn't want to get nipped. Beaver 425
scurried toward the river. He jumped in and swam 434
away from shore. 437

Beaver swam around for a long time. Each time 446
he tried to leave the river, Mother Duck was there, 456
waiting on the banks. Finally, he got very tired of 466
swimming. 467

Beaver found a huge logjam in the river. He 476
dove between the logs and back to the surface. 485
There he found a safe, dry room with a log roof. 496

"Perfect!" said Beaver. "I will live here from 504
now on . . . safe from Mother Duck." 510

The log home worked so well for Beaver that 519
he told his friends about it. And from that day 529
on, beavers have built cozy log homes in rivers 538
and streams. 540

Old, Old Stories

by Sandy Riggs

Why do we have two ears and two eyes but only one mouth? Long ago, Native Americans answered this question by telling this story. A giant named Gluskabe was made by the wind and lightning. The lightning made two holes for Gluskabe's ears and two holes for his eyes. It made only one hole for his mouth. This story means that people should listen twice as much as they should talk. Native Americans believed people could learn many things by listening to stories.

The older people in Native American tribes were important people. They were the ones who told stories. The stories were in their memory. They were not written down. Most of their stories were meant to teach children. From the stories, young people learned the tribe's way of life. They learned the history of their people. The wise old people told and retold the stories. Stories were passed down over many, many years, from one generation to another. The people did not want to forget their history.

Belts

Native American storytellers often used objects to help them remember the stories. One tribe used a kind of belt called wampum. Wampum was made with small white shells. The pattern of the shells showed events.

Bags

Another tribe would use a bag with objects inside. There might be a black feather in the bag. A child might take out the feather. Then the storyteller would tell the story of how Crow got black feathers.

Masks

In other tribes, people made masks for the storytellers. The masks were made of wood. They were the faces of animals such as Bear, Wolf, and Whale. A storyteller would put on one of the masks. Then by the light of a fire, he would tell a story about this animal.

Teepees

Native Americans who lived in teepees painted pictures on the teepees. The grandfathers would tell stories about the great deeds that were pictured. In this way, children would learn the history of their people.

Native Americans are still telling stories to pass on their history to children. Their children are listening with two ears.

The Giant's Bridge

by Rosalie Koskenmaki

If you ever go to Ireland, you should try to visit the Giant's Bridge (or Causeway). It is a great sight. There are two tales of how it came to be. Those who know about such things say it was made when hot, melted rock, called lava, fell into the sea. When the lava cooled, it looked like giant steppingstones. Well, that may be. But here is the other story.

Long ago, in Ireland, there lived a fierce giant named Finn MacCoul. In Scotland, across the sea, lived another fierce giant. His name was Finn Gall. Now, Finn MacCoul wanted to fight Finn Gall. Don't ask why. It's the way giants were.

But how was Finn MacCoul to get to Scotland? 127
It was a long way. The sea was deep. And Finn 138
MacCoul couldn't swim. At last he thought of a 147
way. He set to work. He found many tall stones. 157
He stood them in the sea. He made a road all the 169
way to Finn Gall's place. When he had finished, he 179
was tired. He went home to rest. 186

Now, while he slept, there was a knock on the 196
door. It was Finn Gall! He had found the bridge 206
and crossed it. 209

When Finn MacCoul's wife saw who was at the 218
door, she didn't like it. She could tell that Finn Gall 229
had come to fight. She didn't want a fight in her 240
house. But she was clever, as you will see. 249

Finn Gall looked in the door. He yelled in his 259
huge voice, "Is that MacCoul there on the bed?" It 269
was, of course. 272

"Oh my, no!" said Mrs. MacCoul. "That's our 280
wee baby!" 282

"Is it, now?" said Finn Gall. If the wee baby is 293
that large, he thought, how large must the father 302
be? All of a sudden, he didn't want to fight. 312

So he ran. He ran all the way back to Scotland. 323
And on the way he pulled up as much of the bridge 335
as he could. 338

To this day you can see part of the Giant's 348
Bridge. As to how it got there, you may believe 358
whatever you like. 361

The Lucky Trip

by Lyle Jourdan

Sam was in the kitchen setting the table. He put out the dishes and glasses while Grandma Sarah made lunch. Sam smelled the potatoes and knew they would be tasty. Grandma Sarah made the best lunches ever!

Sam watched his grandmother as she worked. Her bracelet had a tiny airplane and suitcase on it. It made tinny sounds when she stirred the pot. Sam had never seen his grandmother without it.

"Grandma Sarah," Sam asked, "why do you always wear that bracelet?"

Grandma Sarah finished stirring the pot and smiled. "This bracelet is special," she said, "because your Grandpa Mark gave it to me."

"But why the airplane and suitcase?" Sam asked.

"Because of how we met," Grandma Sarah said. "Let me tell you the story."

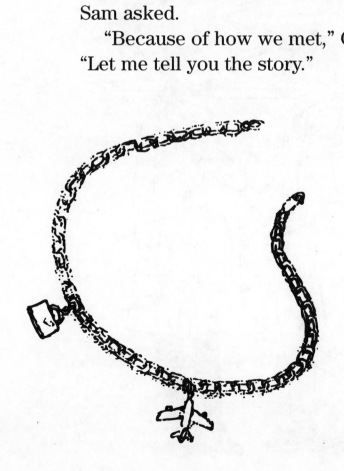

3
6
16
24
32
41
43
50
60
69
77
84
88
95
102
110
116
118
126
132

Grandma Sarah sat down at the table. "I was   141
away from home," she said. "I was flying back to   151
see my parents. When the airplane landed, we all   160
got off and went to get our bags. But it took a very   173
long time for them to come out."   180

"I was lucky because that's when I met your   189
grandfather. He had been on the plane, too. We   198
had to wait two hours for our bags! So we sat on   210
the benches and talked. That was how we met."   219

"What about the bracelet?" Sam asked.   225

"Your grandfather gave it to me to remind me of   235
how we met. And I've never taken it off since!"   245

"What a lucky trip!" Sam cried.   251

Charles Dickens and the Little Children

by Rosalie Koskimaki

3

6

9

Many years ago children from poor families had   17
to work long hours. They had to work very hard.   27
They worked in coal mines and in factories. They   36
didn't earn much money. Their bosses were cruel   44
to them. It was a terrible life for little children.   54
Many of them became ill and died. Some of these   64
children were only seven years old!   70

Charles Dickens wrote books in those days. He   78
felt sorry for the poor little children in England,   87
where he lived. So he wrote a story. It was about a   99
little boy who had to work from morning to night.   109
The boy's name was Oliver Twist. Poor Oliver! All   118
he got to eat every day was three bowls of watery   129
soup. And he had to work so hard!   137

People cried when they read his book. It was a 147
sad story. They knew Oliver wasn't a real little boy. 157
But they also knew there were real boys and girls 167
just like Oliver. These people got busy. They made 176
laws so that children wouldn't have to work so 185
hard. They made laws saying that very young 193
children should not work at all. 199

Nowadays it's against the law to make children 207
work in mines and factories. Charles Dickens 214
helped a lot. His book showed people what a 223
terrible thing was going on. 228

Charles Dickens had a good reason to help 236
those children. He had to go out and work when 246
he was a boy. And he was only ten years old. 257
He never forgot those dreadful days. He wrote 265
his book so that other children could have a 274
better life. 276

A Bee That Isn't a Bug

by Sandy Miller

6

9

A worker bee is a busy insect. Its job is making honey. Many worker bees work together to make the honey. When America was a new country, women sewed quilts. Because there was not much cloth, they used pieces of old clothes. Often the women would get together to sew. They called this a quilting bee. Just like bees, the women were busy working together.

Making the Quilt

The women would stretch a quilt on a frame. Then all the quilters would sit around it. Each person sewed a part of the quilt. The quilting bee was a way to finish a quilt more quickly. The bee was a place for the women to talk with neighbors. They shared ideas, news, and stories. Children would keep the needles threaded.

Sometimes a quilting bee became a quilting party. Guests would come in the evening. Then there would be supper, games, singing, and dancing.

20
28
36
44
53
62
71
74
77
86
95
105
116
126
133
138
145
152
159
161

Little Read Schoolhouse Quilt

165

A Story in Every Quilt

170

Women at a quilting bee would share quilt 178
patterns. The quilt patterns had names. Each name 186
was like a story title. Quilts told stories about the 196
history of America. Some stories were about 203
people moving to new parts of America. One quilt 212
was called Rocky Road to Kansas. It told the story 222
of a time when people had to make roads. It was 233
hard work. They had to move heavy rocks by 242
hand. Another quilt told about the danger of living 251
in a wild place. It was named Bear's Paw. Wives of 262
sea captains told stories with a quilt called All 271
Around the World. 274

There are stories in quilts about how people 282
lived. Quilts showed covered wagons, log cabins, 289
and windmills. Quilts showed the work people did 297
in early America. There were patterns with names 305
like Water Wheel and Saw-tooth. A miller used a 314
water wheel to grind grain into flour. A carpenter 323
used a saw. 326

So if you see a quilt, look at it carefully. It may 338
tell you a story. 342

Water Wheel Quilt   **Saw-tooth Quilt**   347
These patterns tell stories about places.   353

Hard Days and Happy Endings: Frances Hodgson Burnett and *The Little Princess*

One hundred years ago, many children worked. 19
Some worked in the homes of rich people. They 28
cooked and cleaned; they helped with shopping. 35
Life was hard for them. 40

Frances Hodgson Burnett grew up in those 47
days. She didn't have to work for others. But she 57
knew how if felt to be poor. Her father had died 68
when she was five. 72

Frances liked to make up stories. Her sisters 80
loved hearing them. "Write them down!" they said. 88
"Sell them!" So she did. She earned money from 97
her writing. That money helped at home. 104

Frances saw many poor children in her city. 112
They looked tired. She felt sorry for them. So she 122
wrote a book called *The Little Princess*. 129

That book is about Sara. She is nine years old. 139
Her father loses all his money. Then he dies. Sara 149
is poor. She must go to work. 156

Sara must work for rich people. They even have 165
a cook! Sara does housework for them. Here you 174
can read about one of her days: 181

The streets of London were cold and damp. No 190
one wanted to go out on such a day. But Cook 201
needed some things. So she sent Sara. 208

Sara trudged from store to store. Her shoes 216
were soon all wet. Her shabby coat was soaked. 225
She hadn't eaten all day. She was cold, wet, and 235
tired. Most of all, she was hungry. 242

As she often did, Sara made up a story. In the 253
story, she was a princess. Her fur coat and thick 263
boots were warm as toast. She was rich! She 272
could buy candy or a hot drink if she liked. 282

Sara's story made her feel better. At least for 291
a while. 293

Frances Hodgson Burnett gave the book a 300
happy ending. A friend of Sara's father finds Sara. 309
He gives her money. She is rich! At last she is a 321
real princess! 323

The Book of Life

by Andy Green

4
7

Sue was visiting her great-grandfather Opa at
the nursing home. She went there every Sunday.
But today was no ordinary visit. It was special
because it was Sue's birthday. Opa said he had an
unusual gift for her.

"My birthday girl!" Opa cried when Sue entered
his room. He handed her a wrapped box. "This is
for you, dear."

Feeling excited, Sue quickly unwrapped the box
and opened it. Inside was a book. Its cover said
My Life as a Child: A Gift from Opa to Sue.

"I hope you like it," Opa said. "It's a journal I
began writing when I was about your age."

Sue slowly turned the pages. She couldn't
believe how neat Opa's handwriting was. She knew
her own was a little sloppy.

"Thank you, Opa!" Sue cried, hugging him. "I'll
start reading this tonight!"

14
22
31
41
45
53
63
66
73
83
94
105
113
120
128
134
142
146

That night, Sue began to read the journal. This   155
is unbelievable, she thought. Opa's life as a child   164
was so different from her own. In the book he   174
described his school. All the children shared one   182
room and one teacher. Opa had walked three miles   191
to school, too. There were no school buses to   200
ride then.   202

Sue was surprised that there was no television   210
when Opa was young. She thought he would have   219
been unhappy without TV. But instead he seemed   227
quite pleased. He and his friends played lots of   236
games and even made up their own.   243

The next Sunday, Sue returned to the nursing   251
home.   252

"Did you like the book?"   257
Opa asked.   259

"Oh, yes!" Sue said,   263
smiling. "It even gave   267
me an idea." She pulled   272
out a book. The   276
cover said *My Life*   280
as a Child: A Gift   285
from Sue to Opa.   289

Opa said it was one   294
of the best gifts ever.   299

The Storyteller

by Rosalie Koskimaki

Hans Christian Andersen was born long ago in Denmark. His parents were very poor. His father made shoes. But he didn't sell many shoes. So there wasn't much money.

Hans wasn't very happy. And he wasn't very strong. Other children laughed at him. So he didn't like to play with them. Instead, he made up stories. He got his fun from make-believe. He had few friends. When he was eleven, his father died.

But Hans grew up. Things got a little better. He wrote some books. They were for grownups. But then he thought about his boyhood.

"I was a sad little boy," said Hans. "Children shouldn't be sad. I will make up some stories for children. The stories will make them happy."

So Hans wrote four stories for children. They 136
were "The Tinder Box," "Little Claus and Big 144
Claus," "Little Ida's Flowers," and "The Princess 151
and the Pea." 154

Children loved the stories. Even grownups liked 161
them. Hans became famous. He wrote some more 169
stories. He wrote "Thumbelina," "The Emperor's 175
New Clothes," "The Ugly Duckling," and "The Tin 183
Soldier." After that he wrote many more. 190

Many children have read these stories. Hans 197
Christian Andersen did what he said he would do. 206
He made up stories to make children happy. 214
Maybe you'll read some of them. 220

The Country Girl

by Chad Smedley

361 Country Rd.
Plains, NJ 07753

Aug. 1, 1935

Dear Ms. Smith,

I told you I'd write you right after I got to my aunt and uncle's farm. I'm their guest for the last part of summer, and I never guessed the country could be so beautiful!

I get up earlier here than I did for school. In the city I always ate breakfast before eight, but here I'm eating before six! Each morning I raise my window shade and let the sun rays in. I never knew a new day could be so exciting!

The best part of being here is working with all the farm animals. Yesterday I helped shear the wool off two sheep! Did you ever see a ewe before? Sheep are so cute!

Every day I go to the barnyard. There is so much to do there. I help feed all the chicks, ducks, and geese. There is also one cat with furry white hair. Sometimes it follows us around. Most of the time, it is chasing after any mice it sees. I also help my aunt and other women collect eggs in the henhouse.

3
6
9
12
15
18
30
40
49
53
65
74
83
93
101
111
119
129
134
144
155
165
174
186
195
196

My uncle works with the bigger animals. He   204
leads the oxen into the field so they can plow the   215
earth and workers can then sow seeds in the   224
ground. It takes several men to help my uncle get   234
the job done.   237

Tomorrow should be the most exciting day of   245
all! My uncle is going to let me milk a cow! I   257
always knew milk came from a cow, but now I'll   267
be able to see it happening!   273

I can't wait to see you and all the children in   284
school in September!   287

Sincerely,   288

Mary Jane Jones   291

Life on the Prairie

From diaries and letters of pioneer women

adapted by Ben Phillips

4
11
15

Eighty-year-old Annie Clark sits on her porch. She reads from a diary she wrote when she was eight.

22
31
33

May 1, 1861. *Kansas is starting to feel like home. I didn't like it at first. The prairie goes on forever. There are no trees. All I can see is tall grass and animals.*

42
53
64
67

But I love the wildflowers. I pick them and put them in jars. They look bright and cheery. Then our dirt walls don't seem so dark.

77
86
93

It takes a whole day to get to town. My friends live far away. Sometimes I get very lonely.

104
112

July 8, 1861. *I wish it would rain! The grass* 122
is very dry. We always have to watch for fires. 132
Yesterday I saw smoke in the tall grass. I was 142
scared. I knew I had to do something. I wet my 153
petticoat in the stream. Then I beat at the fire. 163
My arms got so tired. But I got every little spark 174
out. Mama and Father were very proud of me. 183

December 21, 1861. *There wasn't any rain* 190
for our crops last summer. Now our food is very 200
low. Father went to Iowa to get corn and wheat. 210
He promised to be home before Mama had the 219
new baby. 221

Today Mama told me the baby was coming. I 230
took care of my little sister. And I kept a fire in 242
the woodstove. I was scared for Mama because 250
Father was not there to help. But now I have a 261
new baby brother. What a surprise for Father! I 270
hope he won't get lost in the snow. 278

Annie closes the diary. She looks out at rows of 288
tall corn. Cows chew lazily on rich green grass. 297
She thinks about her parents. They knew that life 306
would be hard on the prairie. But they believed it 316
was worth it. The land would always be there for 326
their children. 328

The Lost Fawn

by Lena Moore

Jody was strolling along the country hillside. It 14
was a bright afternoon filled with sunshine and a 23
cool breeze. But Jody felt somewhat sad. School 31
was out, and most of his classmates were away for 41
the summer. It was the first time Jody had ever 51
been lonely. 53

Jody watched a jackrabbit that was hopping 60
down the hill. He followed it to a group of bushes 71
in a wooded area nearby. Suddenly Jody saw 79
something move behind one of the bushes. He 87
wasn't sure at first what it was. Jody slowly parted 97
the leaves and peeked through. 102

There stood a pretty baby deer, no more than 111
two feet high. The fawn stared up at Jody, looking 121
sad, lost, and confused. 125

"Where's your mama?" Jody gently asked. 131
"You look puzzled, so I'll tell you what. Why don't 141
you follow me home? You and I can become 150
best friends." 152

Jody began to walk to his farmhouse. Instead of 161
taking large steps, he took tiny footsteps so the 170
fawn could follow. 173

As the two crossed the mountainside, Jody 180
wondered where the fawn had come from. Before 188
he could think much more, a large deer suddenly 197
leaped out of nowhere. The fawn raced to the 206
deer, and the two animals rubbed noses together. 214

Jody smiled. "Here's your mama," he said softly. 222
The two creatures dashed off. Jody knew the fawn 231
would not be his pet. But he still felt good inside. 242

"Perhaps I will meet them again," he said. 250

Reading, Writing, and Teaching!

by Sonia Rojas

2

4

7

Nicaragua is a country in Central America. It is   16
a beautiful place. There are many lakes and   24
mountains. Forests grow tall. But before 1979, half   32
the people in Nicaragua could not read. Most of   41
these people were farmers. They lived in villages   49
far from cities. They had no electricity. They had   58
no roads. They had no schools.   64

The Nicaraguan government wanted to teach   70
the farmers to read. But the government needed   78
teachers to go to the villages. They needed   86
teachers who could learn a different way of life. So   96
they trained young people as teachers. Some of the   105
teachers were teenagers. And some were as young   113
as twelve years old. These young people would be   122
gone for five months. They would miss their   130
families. But these young people were also   137
excited. This was a great adventure for them. And   146
they knew their work was important.   152

One young teacher was Evenor Ortega. He was   160
sixteen years old. Evenor and his group left   168
Managua in April 1980. They went to the villages of   178
San Jose de Bocay. They had to walk miles in   188
steep mountains. A few teachers went to each   196
village. Each teacher stayed with a different family.   204

"Teaching was a real challenge," Ortega said. 211
But almost everyone in the villages wanted to 219
learn to read. Ortega and his group taught children 228
in the mornings. They taught adults in the 236
afternoons. Some of the farmers had never held a 245
book or a pencil before. But they wanted to learn. 255
And they worked hard. First, they learned to write 264
their names. Then, they learned to write words. 272

The teachers learned from their students, too. 279
Ortega learned to plant corn and beans. He also 288
learned about the dangers of the back country. 296
Poisonous snakes lived everywhere. Ortega had to 303
carry a stick to protect himself. 309

Five months passed. Ortega and his group 316
returned to Managua. They were sad to leave their 325
new friends. Almost everyone cried. But the young 333
teachers were proud of themselves. They had done 341
a giant task. They had taught many people to read. 351
"I learned how to give," Ortega said. 358

All About Sheep

by Matt Lyons

3
6
14
24
33
41
44
50
59
67
76
84
92
100
109
118
127
131
137
142
148
153
158
162

Do you think much about sheep? Some people try counting them at night in order to fall asleep. But maybe we should think more about sheep in the daytime. After all, they're among the world's most important animals.

The Benefits and Types of Wool

You benefit from sheep every day, even if you don't realize it. That's because sheep give us wool—the soft, curly hair that grows on their bodies. Wool is used to make many things, including clothes, blankets, and rugs. Wool is a good material because it keeps its shape, doesn't wrinkle, and is easy to clean. Also, it protects against both cold and heat. For all these reasons, wool is often used to make coats, sweaters, gloves, socks, and other items.

There are many kinds of sheep, and they produce many kinds of wool. Some wool is thin, and other wool is thick. Some wool is smooth, and other wool is rough.

The Baa-Baa Shop

165

How is a sheep's wool turned into clothes? It all 175 begins with the shearing, or cutting, of the wool. 184 Think of it as a sheep's "haircut." The wool is cut 195 with "shears," a tool like automatic scissors. 202

Good wool cutters can shear more than 200 210 sheep a day. They remove the wool in one whole 220 piece. Later the wool is cut into halves, and then it 231 is cut into smaller pieces. The best wool grows 240 near the shoulders and sides of the sheep. 248

Sheep are raised and sheared all over the world. 257 In the United States, some sheep are raised on a 267 range—a wide stretch of open land. Each herd has 277 about 1,000 to 2,000 sheep. Other sheep are raised 286 on farms. A farmer might have anywhere from 294 30 to 300 sheep that stay in a fenced pasture. 304

Now, if anyone asks where sheep get a 312 haircut, you'll know. Or, just tell them, "At the 321 baa-baa shop!" 323

The Cowboy's Bandanna

by Ford Jones

Sometimes you wear a scarf round your neck. 14
You may wear it to keep warm. Or you may just 25
like the way it looks. 30

A cowboy wears a scarf too. But he calls 39
it a bandanna. And it has a lot more uses than 50
your scarf. 52

In summer the cowboy's bandanna stops itchy 59
things from getting inside his collar. In winter it 68
keeps his neck warm. He can pull it up to keep his 80
ears warm, too. 83

When the air is dusty, he covers his mouth and 93
nose with the bandanna. It screens some of the 102
dust out of the air. Sometimes he may drink 111
through his bandanna, too. Water will pass through 119
it. Insects and dirt won't. 124

In strong winds he can use it to tie his hat to his   137
head. At night he may tie his horse's feet together   147
with it. Then the horse can't run away.   155

If he wants to sleep in daytime, the cowboy lays   165
the bandanna over his eyes. If something frightens   173
his horse, he may tie it over the horse's eyes.   183
Horses are seldom scared by things they can't see.   192

When a cowboy washes his face, he may dry it   202
with his bandanna. (Cowboys *do* wash their faces,   210
you know.) And if he wears glasses, he may use it   221
to polish them. (Some cowboys *do* wear glasses.)   229

A cowboy may need to bandage a cut with his   239
bandanna. Or he may need it to wrap his food. So   250
he washes it whenever he can. He wants it to be   261
clean. Wouldn't you?   264

Suppose you were a cowboy. How else could   272
you use your bandanna?   276

Who Were the Shakers?

by Susan Alcorn

Have you ever seen how seeds are sold? Flower and vegetable seeds are packed in small envelopes with a picture on the front and planting directions on the back. But seeds weren't always sold this way.

Many years ago people sold seeds from a big barrel. It was hard to count the number of seeds you were getting. It was hard to know how much to pay. Then a group called the Shakers had the idea of putting just a few seeds in those small paper envelopes we see today.

Who were these Shakers? The first Shakers came to America from England in 1774. They came looking for a better life. They moved to small towns in the country and set up what were called Shaker villages.

The Shaker Inventions

In the big cities there were lots of stores where you could buy whatever you needed. But in the country, the Shakers had to learn to do everything for themselves. They built their own houses. They sewed their own clothes. They made their own furniture. They grew all the food they ate. And besides packaged seeds, the Shakers also created the flat broom, the clothespin, a special washing machine, and many other useful tools and inventions.

4
7
16
24
33
41
43
52
62
72
82
92
97
104
113
122
132
134
137
147
156
165
173
181
190
197
205
212
213

The first thing other people noticed when they   221
entered a Shaker house was how neat and simple   230
it was. The Shakers believed in living a simple and   240
plain life. There were hardly any ornaments or   248
decorations on display. And everything was in its   256
place. The Shakers even hung their chairs from the   265
wall to make it easier to keep the floors clean.   275
You'd never find a messy room in a Shaker house.   285

The Shaker Museums   288

The Shakers were not allowed to marry. To   296
continue growing, they let people from the nearby   304
towns join up and become Shakers. Shakers also   312
took in children who had lost a mother or father   322
and had no one to take care of them. Later, when   333
they grew up, many of these children decided to   342
become Shakers. One interesting thing you can   349
learn at the museums is how the Shakers got their   359
name. They used to dance and shake at their   368
prayer meetings.   370

At one time, there were over 6,000 Shakers in   379
America. Today there are fewer than a dozen left.   388
But you can learn about the way they lived by   398
visiting a Shaker museum.   402

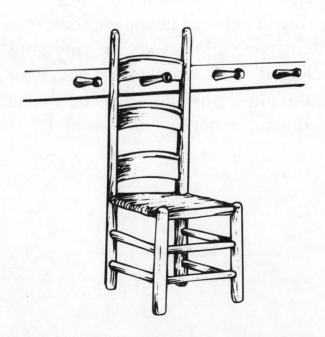

It Could Be Worse!

(based on a story by Sholem Aleichem)

by Kenneth Lloyd

Abraham lived in a small village. He owned a little land where he raised some vegetables. In his yard, he kept a cow, a nanny goat with two kids, and a few chickens. Abraham should have been a happy man. He wasn't rich, but he had more than many of his fellow villagers.

But Abraham was miserable.

Much of the time, he went around complaining. He complained to his friends. He complained to anyone who would listen. Abraham's big complaint was his house.

Abraham's house had only one small room. In that room, Abraham lived, cooked, ate, and slept. Just about everything Abraham did took place in that room.

Abraham spent much of his time outside, 130
tending to his vegetables and animals. But each 138
time he went back to his house, he would look out 149
his one small window. He would think about living 158
in a huge dwelling with many rooms. The more he 168
thought, the worse he felt. The worse he felt, the 178
more he complained. 181

"Abraham, stop complaining!" ordered his 186
neighbor, Saul. "We are sick and tired of hearing 195
about how small your house is. Why don't you just 205
make it bigger!" 208

"Hah!" cried Abraham. "And what am I 215
supposed to use for money? Do you think I am a 226
wealthy man?" 228

"Well, go and ask the village wise man what to 238
do," advised Saul. "You will have no friends left if 248
you keep complaining." 251

So, Abraham went to see the village wise man. 260
Abraham told about his land and animals. He 268
complained about his too-small house. 273

The wise man listened attentively to all of 281
Abraham's complaints. "Abraham, you must 286
promise me that you will do exactly what I say for 297
ten days. Then, you must come back and tell me 307
what happened." 309

"Anything!" promised Abraham. "All right, then," 315
said the wise man. "Go home and take all your 325
animals into your house. Let them out only when 334
you are working on your land. Anytime you are in 344
the house, the animals must be there with you. Do 354
you understand?" "Yes," said Abraham weakly. He 361
didn't understand at all. But he had promised the 370
wise man that he would do what he was told. 380

Abraham shuffled home, his shoulders 385
drooping. He gathered up the cow, the goat and 394
her kids, and the chickens. Into the house they 403
all went. 405

Abraham could hardly move about inside his 412
tiny house. Once, he accidentally stepped on the 420
cow's tail. With a great moo, she got up and kicked 431
over his table. 434

The goat chewed off one leg of Abraham's bed. 443
The chickens ran about cackling and pecking at 451
Abraham's toes. 453

At the end of ten days, Abraham rushed back to 463
the wise man. "You didn't solve my problem," he 472
cried. "You made it worse!" 477

The wise man didn't seem surprised. "We are 485
not yet finished," he said calmly. "Go home now 494
and put all the animals back outside." 501

Abraham hurried home and did as the wise man 510
said. Then, he swept out the chicken feathers and 519
fixed the leg of his bed. Finally, he looked around 529
his house. The wise man was right! The room 538
seemed twice as large as it had before! 546

Abraham had learned a very important lesson. 553
No matter how bad something seems . . . it could 561
always be worse! 564

The Hoarse Horse

by Bill Overman

3

6

13

24

32

41

50

57

66

77

80

89

97

106

114

118

124

132

141

145

Everyone in the countryside was getting ready for the big contest. It was a horse race that took place each year in August. Folks from miles around came to the raceway to watch. The riders were farm kids who rode horses they helped to raise and train. The winner won $100.

Marta was excited about being a rider this year. She knew the race was new to her but felt she could still win.

On the morning of the race, Marta visited her horse. Rusty was quietly eating hay and seemed unaware of the big contest. Seeing Marta, he cried, "Neigh!" Marta heard an unusual sound and turned to Ed, the trainer.

"Rusty's voice seems strange," she said.

"He's a little hoarse," Ed explained. "His voice was weak last week. But it's better now. It shouldn't hurt his racing."

Later, Marta and Ed led Rusty to the starting   154
gate. A bell rang, and the race began. The horses   164
took off, and rows of dust clouds rose in the air.   175

To Marta's surprise, Rusty refused to move.   182
"Come on, boy!" she cried, but Rusty stood   190
motionless.   191

Suddenly, Rusty began to run, but not on the   200
track. Instead he raced to a nearby lake and took a   211
long drink that seemed endless.   216

Finally, Rusty was ready to race. He returned   224
to the track and began to trot. Marta rode him   234
down the track as fast as she could. Rusty quickly   244
picked up speed and soon had caught up with the   254
other horses.   256

With unbelievable speed, Rusty passed the other   263
horses and then ran past the finish line. Marta and   273
Rusty had won!   276

"Looks like our hoarse horse knew just how to   285
get to the finish line," Ed said. "That Rusty has   295
horse sense!"   297

A Slice of Tree Trunk

by Ruth C. Parker

John's Uncle Ted stopped the car. "Here's a good place for our picnic," he said. They got out. They sat on a fallen tree trunk.

"The woods are nice," said John. "I wish we lived in the woods."

"Long ago, people did," said Uncle Ted. "But they had to work hard. They had to hunt for food. They had to build fires. Life wasn't easy."

"How did they do it all?"

"They thought up things to help them. Once they had to carry everything themselves. Or they'd drag things behind them. Then they thought of an easier way. What do you think they made?"

"Wagons?" asked John.   116

"First they needed wheels," said Uncle Ted.   123

"Didn't they even know about wheels?" asked   130
John. "How did they think of them?"   137

"Look at this tree trunk," said Uncle Ted. "What   146
would a slice of it look like?"   153

John looked. A man could cut a slice of tree   163
trunk. It would be round. And it would roll.   172

"Was that the first wheel?" John asked.   179

"Most likely," answered his uncle. "It was just a   188
slice of tree trunk. But it was one of the most   199
useful things any man ever made.   205

"Later on, people learned to make better   212
wheels. Then wagons ran better. Work got easier."   220

"Now we have wheels on lots of things," said   229
John. "We have wheels on trains and bicycles and   238
planes. We came here today on wheels!"   245

"And it all started with a slice of tree trunk."   255

"May I have a slice?" asked John.   262

"A slice of tree trunk?"   267

"No—a slice of cake," said John, reaching into   276
the picnic basket.   279

The Bravest Sheepdog

by Amelia La Croix

3
7

Pete sat outside in the meadow, watching the sheep. It seemed like the hottest day of the year. Even sitting under a large tree, Pete found the heat very hard to take.

Pete wasn't alone with the flock. Shep, the family sheepdog, helped him. Shep was the gentlest, friendliest, and smartest dog that Pete had ever known. Pete smiled as he watched Shep run around the meadow, seeing that none of the sheep wandered away.

Pete counted and then recounted the sheep to make sure they were all there. Neighbors had sent recent warnings of sheep attacks. This meant wolves were in the area.

As the time passed, Pete grew hotter. He decided to go inside the house for a while to cool off.

Inside, Pete lay down on the couch and soon   140
fell asleep. Meanwhile, in the meadow, two wolves   148
quietly made their way to the fence that   156
surrounded the yard. They appeared, briefly   162
disappeared in the bushes, and then reappeared.   169
They leaped over the fence and slowly approached   177
the flock.   179

Shep saw the wolves and began barking loudly.   187
Bravely he stood between the sheep and the   195
wolves, refusing to take even one step back.   203

The wolves inched closer, but Shep stood his   211
ground. As he barked fiercely, the house door   219
suddenly opened, and Pete came running out. The   227
wolves turned and quickly ran away.   233

"Oh, Shep!" Pete cried. "You're not just the   241
gentlest, friendliest, and smartest sheepdog ever.   247
You're also the bravest!"   251

An Author Who Cares

by Rachel Hiatt

Do you remember your first day of school? How did you feel? Were you excited? Were you afraid?

Dolores Johnson is an adult. But she remembers how she felt on her first day of school. She can recall her feelings at other times, too. She remembers how she felt having a new babysitter. She remembers living with a stepparent. She remembers feeling scared the first time she stayed home alone.

Dolores writes and illustrates children's stories. She knows that children today probably have the very same feelings she had. They probably worry about the very same things that she worried about. So she writes stories about these problems. The characters in her stories have the same problems that real children have.

Dolores wants children to know everyone feels 135
afraid or sad or worried at certain times. That's 144
why she writes about children who have these 152
feelings. One book she wrote is called *What Will* 161
Mommy Do When I Go to School? The main 170
character is a girl. She is about to start school. Is 181
she worried? Of course! But she pretends she is 190
afraid that her mother will be lonely. 197

Another book is *Papa's Stories*. The main 204
character is a girl named Kari. She discovers her 213
dad hasn't been honest about something. And so 221
she worries that he is also lying about loving her. 231

Dolores wasn't always a writer. She started out 239
as an artist. She made stained glass windows. She 248
painted pictures. She made clay into bowls. Then 256
Dolores decided to take a writing course. She 264
learned how to put her feelings into words. After 273
five years of hard work, Dolores sold her first 282
book. Since that time, Dolores has sold many 290
more books. 292

"When I was a child, I never saw children in 302
books that looked like me," said Dolores, an 310
African-American. That's why many characters in 316
her books are African-American. But she writes 323
about topics that "all children can relate to, no 332
matter what race they are." 337

Dolores Johnson wants children to feel good 344
about themselves. She hopes her books help make 352
that happen. 354

Belling the Cat

retold by Jeff Weller

3
7

On a country farm, there once lived a family of   17
mice. They mostly led joyful lives, running freely   25
around the barn. Their days were filled with peace   34
and happiness.   36

There were times, though, when things were not   44
so peaceful. Those times came when the cat   52
suddenly showed up by surprise. The cat was large   61
and fierce. What a frightful sight she was to the   71
poor mice! She would chase them out of the barn   81
and through the fields. The mice had to use their   91
quickness to stay one step ahead of that awful cat.   101

One day, the mice met to talk about their cat   111
problem. One mouse had an idea. "We should run   120
the cat off the farm!" the mouse said.   128

"We can't," another mouse said. "The cat is too   137
powerful to chase away. She seems to have no   146
weakness at all. Any other ideas?"   152

Finally, another mouse spoke up. "Let's tie a 160
bell around the cat's neck, so she won't be able to 171
surprise us. If we hear the bell ringing, we'll know 181
the cat is nearby. That'll give us ample time to 191
run away." 193

The other mice liked the idea. "Delightful!" they 201
cried. "Bell the cat, bell the cat! There'll be no 211
more sadness once we've belled the cat!" 218

Finally, one mouse spoke up. "It all sounds 226
fine," he said, "but one small piece of business 235
remains. Who will tie the bell on the cat's neck? 245
Who is willing to get that close?" 252

Suddenly, all was quiet. The mice looked at 260
each other with sorrowful eyes. None of them had 269
the braveness to bell the cat. 275

That day, the mice learned an important lesson. 283
An idea is good only if it really works. After all, 294
easier said than done! 298

Paul Bunyan and the Great Lakes

(an original tall tale)

by Nancy Sladky

If you look on a map of North America, you'll see a string of lakes between the United States and Canada. Known as the Great Lakes, they are the largest group of freshwater lakes in the world. Judging by their size, it's no mystery why they are considered great. But explaining how they got that way is another story.

According to people living in the north woods, Paul Bunyan created these lakes. Paul Bunyan was a giant lumberjack. He was very large and strong. He could chop down an entire forest in a single afternoon and saw the lumber into boards by nightfall. In fact, Paul cleared the trees from North Dakota and South Dakota so people could farm the land.

Paul Bunyan's best friend was a giant blue ox   143
named Babe. Paul and Babe made a fine team.   152
Paul swung the ax and cut timber with a bucksaw, 162
and Babe hauled the logs away. It was a good idea 173
to stay far away from the two when they were   183
working. Sawdust flew, wood chips rained down,   190
and logs tipped over like toothpicks. It was very 199
impressive. There wasn't a lumberjack around who 206
could hold a candle to Paul Bunyan.   213

When the two weren't working, you could find   221
Paul and Babe either eating, sleeping, or playing 229
jokes on each other. More than anything, they   237
loved to laugh and throw each other around in   246
huge wrestling matches. Once, after a match in   254
Madison, Wisconsin, Babe fell a bit too hard.   262
The ground shook. Paul thought the townspeople   269
would become very angry when they saw the   277
hole Babe had made in the middle of their town.   287
"We're in really hot water this time," Paul told 296
Babe. But it wasn't so. Rain filled up the hole, and 307
the people of Madison had themselves a place to   316
swim and sail.   319

There usually wasn't much time for play,   326
because Paul and Babe spent a lot of time eating. 336
Every day, Paul ate three square meals. Breakfast 344
was his favorite. Each morning, Paul cooked a   352
lumberjack's breakfast. It consisted of a stack of 360
pancakes higher than a pine tree, a truckload of 369
fried potatoes, and several buckets of juice.   376

Babe liked to eat, too. Paul always shared his   385
food with Babe. That is, except for one time. On   395
this day, Paul worked especially hard and fell   403
asleep before feeding Babe. Babe was starving!   410
When he heard Paul's loud snoring, he knew there   419
wouldn't be a big, tasty dinner. Instead, he'd have 428
to eat plain, old hay—which he did.   436

Babe grew very thirsty after eating that hay. He   445
rushed to the river and drank the whole thing dry. 455
But this wasn't enough. He was still thirsty, and   464
the water was gone. Babe became so thirsty, he   473
couldn't stand up.   476

The next morning, Paul found Babe lying on   484
the ground. Paul could tell Babe needed more   492
water. He grabbed his shovel and started digging. 500
He figured that he would strike water if he dug   510
deep enough.   512

Well, sure enough, by midday, Paul struck   519
water. He kept digging until the hole was so deep 529
it formed a lake. Today, we call that watering hole 539
Lake Superior. But Babe was still thirsty. So Paul 548
dug three more watering holes—Lake Michigan,   555
Lake Huron, and Lake Erie.   560

Babe was so happy that he drank himself blue.   569
Then, to have a little fun, Babe threw Paul into the 580
water. The enormous splash created the fifth Great 588
Lake—Lake Ontario. And that's how the Great Lakes 597
came to be.   600

Worksheets

Common and Proper Nouns

**Read the story and circle letters that should be capitalized.
Write the correct letter above each circle. Then write the story
correctly on the lines below.**

Rosa and ⓣed play soccer. Their team is the ⓡockets. They practice
on Wednesdays. They play games on Saturdays. Last week they battled
the ⓣigers at ⓢun Park. Rosa made a goal. Ted did not make a goal, but
he stole the ball from the ⓣigers. The Rockets won!

This week Ted and Rosa want to beat the ⓙets. They have a plan.
Rosa will pass the ball to Ted. He will kick it into the net for a goal.

Rosa and Ted play soccer. Their team is the
Rockets. They practice on Wednesdays. They
play games on Saturdays. Last week they battled
the Tigers at Sun Park. Rosa made a goal. Ted
did not make a goal, but he stole the ball from
the Tigers. The Rockets won!

This week Ted and Rosa want to beat the Jets.
They have a plan. Rosa will pass the ball to Ted.
He will kick it into the net for a goal.

_____

UNIT I   Friendship • **Lesson 2** *Angel Child, Dragon Child*

Pronouns

Read each sentence and circle each pronoun.

1. (They) will play the drums.

2. (She) will twirl a baton.

3. Murray called (us.)

4. Jan wants (me) to play the cymbals.

5. (I) think the parade will be wonderful.

Read each pair of sentences. Write the pronoun from the second sentence of each pair on the line. Then write the noun from the first sentence on the second line.

1. The parade is coming. It is noisy.

       It   **parade**

2. The children are ready. They are dressed up.

      They   **children**

3. The audience sees Chris. People watch her.

      her   **Chris**

UNIT 1   Friendship • **Lesson 3** *The Tree House*

Linking Verbs

Read each sentence. Circle each linking verb.

1. My name (is) Maxine.

2. Today (is) a fun costume day at school.

3. My costume (is) an astronaut costume.

4. I (was) an astronaut last year too.

5. My two sisters (are) twins.

6. Last year they (were) twin ballerinas.

7. This year they (are) twin clowns.

8. The three of us (are) friends.

9. There (were) many parents handing out treats.

10. The party (was) fun last year.

UNIT I Friendship • **Lesson 4** *Rugby and Rosie*

Verb Phrases

**Read each sentence to yourself. Underline the verb phrase.
Circle the main verb and put a check mark above the
helping verbs.**

1. I wish I could (go) to the zoo.

2. You should (buy) that sweater.

3. We were (planning) on leaving tomorrow.

4. We might have (won) the prize, but we won't (know) until Monday.

UNIT I   Friendship • **Lesson 4** *Rugby and Rosie*

Verbs

Read each sentence. Underline the main verb and its helping verb.

1. My hands <u>are resting</u> on the workbench.

2. They <u>have worked</u> hard.

3. I <u>am looking</u> at them.

4. One knuckle <u>is coated</u> with clay.

5. One finger <u>is covered</u> with paint.

6. I <u>have made</u> a beautiful vase.

7. I <u>will give</u> this wonderful present to my mom.

8. Jess and Thelma <u>are making</u> an unusual art project.

9. They <u>will paint</u> with their feet.

10. Jess <u>will mix</u> the paint.

Kinds of Sentences

Read each sentence and put the correct punctuation at the end.

1. Are you going to the library after our science class?

2. Our team has practiced for two weeks.

3. Should we continue to practice?

4. My, this meal looks delicious!

5. Use good manners when you eat.

6. She is a fast runner but not as fast as Susan.

8. Ouch, these plates are really hot!

9. Our gym teacher has arranged these games.

10. Clear the plates from the table.

Kinds of Sentences

Read the story and circle each incorrect end mark. Write the correct end mark above each circle. Then write the story correctly on the lines below.

Penny can't find her puppy?

"Have you seen my dog." she asks over and over. No one has seen

little Muffin?

Rick sees how sad Penny feels? He decides to help look for Muffin!

"Look." Rick calls. "Here is Muffin under the porch?"

Penny runs to Rick and grabs Muffin. "Muffin, you silly dog?"

Penny cries. "Thanks, Rick?" says Penny as she walks Muffin home.

Penny can't find her puppy.

"Have you seen my dog?" she asks over and over. No one has seen little Muffin.

Rick sees how sad Penny feels. He decides to help look for Muffin. "Look!" Rick calls. "Here is Muffin under the porch."

Penny runs to Rick and grabs Muffin. "Muffin, you silly dog!" Penny cries. "Thanks, Rick!" says Penny as she walks Muffin home.

Name_____ Date _____

Review

Read each sentence. Write interrogative, declarative, imperative, or explanatory on the line following each sentence.

1. Don't shout at me. _____ imperative _____

2. Ouch, that hurt! _____ exclamatory _____

3. I want a dog for my birthday. _____ declarative _____

4. Did you say you bought that book? _____ interrogative _____

Read each sentence. Underline the nouns, circle the verb phrase, and put a check mark above each pronoun in the sentences.

1. The cow (was eating) the green grass.

2. ✔ I (am going) to go to the store in the morning.

3. The dog (is barking) loudly at the children.

4. The old lady (is sitting) on the front porch.

5. ✔ She (is knitting) a wool sweater.

Quotation Marks and Dialogue

Read the story and put an arrow wherever quotation marks are needed. Put quotation marks above the arrow. Then write the story correctly on the lines below.

"Who will help me mix milk and sugar?" asked Mrs. Potter.

"Not I," said Dog.

"Who will help me get ice?" asked Mrs. Potter.

"Not I," said Cat.

"Who will help me eat ice cream?" asked Mrs. Potter.

"We will," said Dog and Cat.

"No, I will eat it all myself," said Mrs. Potter.

"Who will help me mix milk and sugar?"
asked Mrs. Potter.

"Not I," said Dog.

"Who will help me get ice?" asked Mrs. Potter.

"Not I," said Cat.

"Who will help me eat ice cream?" asked
Mrs. Potter.

"We will," said Dog and Cat.

"No, I will eat it all myself," said Mrs. Potter.

_____

Quotation Marks and Dialogue

Read the story and put an arrow wherever quotation marks are needed. Put quotation marks above the arrow. Then write the story correctly on the lines below.

Tina went to the store.

"I am here to get a present for my mother," she said.

"What does your mother like?" asked the shopkeeper.

Tina told the shopkeeper, "She likes books and music."

"Look around for something you think she would like. We have many books and CDs," said the shopkeeper.

"I think I will take this CD," decided Tina.

Tina went to the store.

"I am here to get a present for my mother," she said.

"What does your mother like?" asked the shopkeeper.

Tina told the shopkeeper, "She likes books and music."

"Look around for something you think she would like. We have many books and CDs," said the shopkeeper.

"I think I will take this CD," decided Tina.

Quotation Marks and Dialogue

Read the sentences below. Draw arrows wherever quotation marks are needed and insert any necessary punctuation marks above the space where they should be placed. Then rewrite the sentences correctly on the lines below.

"I would like to play outside" said Gina.

"I know" answered her mother "But right now isn't a good time"

"Why not?" Gina asked.

"Because it is raining" replied her mother. "You can help me make a

pie if you want."

"That sounds like fun" said Gina.

"I would like to play outside," said Gina.

"I know," answered her mother. "But right now isn't a good time."

"Why not?" Gina asked.

"Because it is raining," replied her mother. "You can help me make a pie if you want."

"That sounds like fun," said Gina.

UNIT 2   City Wildlife • **Lesson 2** *City Critters: Wild Animals Live in Cities, Too*

Commas in a Series

Read the story and put an arrow wherever a comma is needed. Place the comma above the arrow. Then write the story correctly on the lines below.

Ali had crayons, scissors, and tape. He wanted to draw, color, and cut. He would make cards for Tom, Ben, Pasha, and Mom. He would make silly monsters for Pasha, Ben, and Tom. He would make pretty flowers for Mom. He drew monster faces, arms, and legs. He drew pretty flowers. Then he colored them and cut them out. Ali taped monsters to the cards for his friends. He taped red, purple, and yellow flowers to Mom's card. Then he gave the cards to Tom, Ben, Pasha, and Mom.

Ali had crayons, scissors, and tape. He wanted to draw, color, and cut. He would make cards for Tom, Ben, Pasha, and Mom. He would make silly monsters for Pasha, Ben, and Tom. He would make pretty flowers for Mom. He drew monster faces, arms, and legs. He drew pretty flowers. Then he colored them and cut them out. Ali taped monsters to the cards for his friends. He taped red, purple, and yellow flowers to Mom's card. Then he gave the cards to Tom, Ben, Pasha, and Mom.

UNIT 2   City Wildlife • **Lesson 2** *City Critters: Wild Animals*
                        Live in Cities, Too

Commas in a Series

Read the story and put an arrow wherever a comma is needed. Place the comma above the arrow. Then write the story correctly on the lines below.

Chip, Cheep, and Champ were mice. They had a nice hole where they could eat, sleep, and play. But the cat was always sniffing, pawing, and scratching at their hole.

"If we put a bell on the cat, it would ring, jingle, and clang when the cat comes near," they said.

But they didn't have a bell, or a collar, or a string to tie it on to the cat's neck. So they just had to be careful when they went out.

Chip, Cheep, and Champ were mice. They had

a nice hole where they could eat, sleep, and play.

But the cat was always sniffing, pawing, and

scratching at their hole.

"If we put a bell on the cat, it would ring, jingle,

and clang when the cat comes near," they said.

But they didn't have a bell, or a collar, or a

string to tie it on to the cat's neck. So they just

had to be careful when they went out.

_____

_____

UNIT 2 City Wildlife • **Lesson 2** *City Critters: Wild Animals
Live in Cities, Too*

Commas in a Series

Read the story and put an arrow wherever a comma is needed. Place the comma above the arrow. Then write the story correctly on the lines below.

I have noticed lots of wildlife in my neighborhood. Some of the wild animals I see are mice, raccoons, and squirrels. The squirrels are my favorite to watch. They scurry, scamper, and play together. Some of the wildlife I see is plants and trees. I am beginning to recognize the different types. So far, I can identify pokeberry plants, sycamore trees, and maple trees. I want to learn the names of other types of wildlife as well.

I have noticed lots of wildlife in my neighborhood. Some of the wild animals I see are mice, raccoons, and squirrels. The squirrels are my favorite to watch. They scurry, scamper, and play together. Some of the wildlife I see is plants and trees. I am beginning to recognize the different types. So far, I can identify pokeberry plants, sycamore trees, and maple trees. I want to learn the names of other types of wildlife as well.

UNIT 2   City Wildlife • **Lesson 3** *Make Way for Ducklings*

Commas in Dialogue

Read the following sentences and put an arrow wherever a comma is needed. Place the comma above the arrow. Then write the sentences correctly on the lines below.

1. Beth called "Hurry or we'll be late."

   Beth called, "Hurry or we'll be late."

2. "That pony is mine" Carla stated.

   "That pony is mine," Carla stated.

3. Eric said "I have a new puppy."

   Eric said, "I have a new puppy."

4. Brent yelled "Look out!"

   Brent yelled, "Look out!"

5. "Time to get up" called Mom.

   "Time to get up," called Mom.

6. The bus driver asked "Is this your stop?"

   The bus driver asked, "Is this your stop?"

7. "You can borrow my bike" offered Matt.

   "You can borrow my bike," offered Matt.

8. "That is a pretty flower" Gina noted.

   "That is a pretty flower," Gina noted.

Commas in Dialogue

Read the following sentences and put an arrow wherever a comma is needed. Place the comma above the arrow. Then write the sentences correctly on the lines below.

1. Carol asked,"Where are my keys?"

   Carol asked, "Where are my keys?"

2. "I want to go first," Jesse called.

   "I want to go first," Jesse called.

3. My father said,"Please clean your room now."

   My father said, "Please clean your room now."

4. "That is a beautiful sunset," Mom observed.

   "That is a beautiful sunset," Mom observed.

5. "Let's leave right now," said Misha.

   "Let's leave right now," said Misha.

6. Jeff wondered,"What will the weather be like on Saturday?"

   Jeff wondered, "What will the weather be like on Saturday?"

7. Emma said,"I have the greatest friends."

   Emma said, "I have the greatest friends."

8. Keith shouted,"Run, Matt, run!"

   Keith shouted, "Run, Matt, run!"

Commas in Dialogue

Read the following sentences and put an arrow wherever a comma is needed. Place the comma above the arrow. Then write the sentences correctly on the lines below.

1. Bill asked, "Where is the city library?"

   Bill asked, "Where is the city library?"

2. "That is the tallest building I have ever seen," gasped Maria.

   "That is the tallest building I have ever seen," gasped Maria.

3. "I would like to see the mountains," said Steven.

   "I would like to see the mountains," said Steven.

4. "Don't forget your jacket," called Mary.

   "Don't forget your jacket," called Mary.

5. John called out, "Here, Sparky! Here, boy!"

   John called out, "Here, Sparky! Here, boy!"

6. "You're going to win the race," Carol stated.

   "You're going to win the race," Carol stated.

Capitalization of Proper Place Names

Read the following sentences and circle the place names that should be capitalized. Write the capital letter above the circle. Then copy the sentences correctly on the lines below.

1. My mother is the librarian at the peninsula public library.
   P   P   L

   My mother is the librarian at the Peninsula

   Public Library.

2. Jeff's grandparents are from boston, massachusetts.
   B   M

   Jeff's grandparents are from Boston,

   Massachusetts.

3. Stephen was born in england.
   E

   Stephen was born in England.

4. We took a vacation to yosemite national park.
   Y   N   P

   We took a vacation to Yosemite National Park.

5. Dad works at the building around the corner.

   Dad works at the building around the corner.

6. The golden gate bridge is beautiful.
   G   G   B

   The Golden Gate Bridge is beautiful.

7. I once lived in new york.
   N   Y

   I once lived in New York.

UNIT 2   City Wildlife • **Lesson 4** *Urban Roosts: Where Birds Nest in the City*

Capitalization of Proper Place Names

Read the following sentences and circle the place names that should be capitalized. Write the capital letter above the circle. Then copy the sentences correctly on the lines below.

1. The ⓢsears tower is in ⓒchicago.

   The Sears Tower is in Chicago.

2. We love to visit ⓢspain and ⓟportugal.

   We love to visit Spain and Portugal.

3. The wind blew through the city and the bridge swayed.

   The wind blew through the city and the

   bridge swayed.

4. Juan has been to the ⓖgrand ⓒcanyon six times!

   Juan has been to the Grand Canyon six times!

5. Would you like to visit ⓜmiami, ⓕflorida?

   Would you like to visit Miami, Florida?

6. My favorite amusement park is ⓓdisney ⓦworld.

   My favorite amusement park is Disney World.

UNIT 2 City Wildlife • **Lesson 4** *Urban Roosts: Where Birds Nest in the City*

Capitalization of Proper Place Names

Read the following sentences and circle the place names that should be capitalized. Write the capital letter above the circle. Then copy the sentences correctly on the lines below.

1. Have you ever been to (idaho?)

   Have you ever been to Idaho?

2. The picnic will be held at (schiller park.)

   The picnic will be held at Schiller Park.

3. Which state do you like best?

   Which state do you like best?

4. Mom wants to go to (yellowstone national park) this summer.

   Mom wants to go to Yellowstone National Park this summer.

5. The park looked beautiful in the spring.

   The park looked beautiful in the spring.

6. The (smith brothers building) is going to be torn down.

   The Smith Brothers Building is going to be torn down.

Exclamation Points and Question Marks

Read the following sentences and add the correct end punctuation to each one. Then copy the sentences correctly on the lines below.

1. What do you want to do today**?**

   What do you want to do today? _____

2. Is Julie related to you**?**

   Is Julie related to you? _____

3. Watch out**!**

   Watch out! _____

4. What time does the movie start**?**

   What time does the movie start? _____

5. Give me my crayons, now**!**

   Give me my crayons, now! _____

6. Oscar hit a grand slam**!**

   Oscar hit a grand slam! _____

7. Who would like to help plan the party**?**

   Who would like to help plan the party? _____

8. Why does your sister wear that funny hat**?**

   Why does your sister wear that funny hat? _____

Exclamation Points and Question Marks

Read the following sentences and add the correct end punctuation to each one. Then copy the sentences correctly on the lines below.

1. The Giants won the basketball game!

   The Giants won the basketball game!_____

2. A hurricane is coming!

   A hurricane is coming!_____

3. Where is the cafeteria?

   Where is the cafeteria?_____

4. Could I have a glass of water, please?

   Could I have a glass of water, please?_____

5. When will it be time to go to Grandma's house?

   When will it be time to go to Grandma's_____

   house?_____

6. What beautiful work you do!

   What beautiful work you do!_____

7. What is your favorite type of cookie?

   What is your favorite type of cookie?_____

8. My house is on fire!

   My house is on fire!_____

Exclamation Points and Question Marks

Read the following sentences and add the correct end punctuation to each one. Then copy the sentences correctly on the lines below.

1. Don't drop that pan!

   Don't drop that pan! _____

2. What is the temperature?

   What is the temperature? _____

3. Our projects are due on Friday.

   Our projects are due on Friday. _____

4. Who knows the answer to this question?

   Who knows the answer to this question? _____

5. Look at that huge bird!

   Look at that huge bird! _____

6. Which desk is yours?

   Which desk is yours? _____

7. Look out for that big wave!

   Look out for that big wave! _____

8. Do you know where the Millers live?

   Do you know where the Millers live? _____

UNIT 2   City Wildlife • **Lesson 6** *Secret Place*

Quotation Marks and Dialogue

Read the story. Place arrows where quotation marks or commas are needed. Put the quotation marks or comma above each arrow. Then write the dialogue correctly on the lines below.

Bill said,"I have saved seven dollars."

Mary said,"I have six dollars in my piggy bank."

"I have three dollars in my pocket and two dollars at home,"

Paul said.

"I want to earn three more dollars. Then I can buy a new book

about dinosaurs," said Bill.

Mary said,"I spent five dollars last week. I bought a present for

my sister."

   Bill said, "I have saved seven dollars."

   Mary said, "I have six dollars in my piggy bank."

   "I have three dollars in my pocket and two

dollars at home," Paul said.

   "I want to earn three more dollars. Then I can

buy a new book about dinosaurs," said Bill.

   Mary said, "I spent five dollars last week. I

bought a present for my sister."

Name_____ Date_____

Quotation Marks and Dialogue

Read the story. Place arrows where quotation marks or commas are needed. Put the quotation marks or comma above each arrow. Then write the dialogue correctly on the lines below.

"I want to live in the city," said Scott.

"I like the country better," said Marla.

Scott said, "I like the tall buildings and the excitement."

"I like to be where it is quiet," said Marla, "and where I can hear birds

singing."

"I guess we just like different things," said Scott.

"I guess so," said Marla, "but does that mean we can't be friends?"

___"I want to live in the city," said Scott.___

___"I like the country better," said Marla.___

___Scott said, "I like the tall buildings and the___

___excitement."___

___"I like to be where it is quiet," said Marla, "and___

___where I can hear birds singing."___

___"I guess we just like different things," said___

___Scott.___

___"I guess so," said Marla, "but does that mean___

___we can't be friends?"___

Quotation Marks and Dialogue

Read the story. Place arrows where quotation marks or commas are needed. Put the quotation marks or comma above each arrow. Then write the dialogue correctly on the lines below.

"Did you hear that?" asked Debbie.

"Hear what?" replied Chris.

"That rustling noise in the bushes," Debbie answered.

"Oh, no!" cried Chris. "I know what that must be."

"What is it then?" asked Debbie.

"I left our trash bag outside. Now a raccoon has gotten into it," said Chris.

"What a mess that will be!" exclaimed Debbie.

"Did you hear that?" asked Debbie.

"Hear what?" replied Chris.

"That rustling noise in the bushes," Debbie answered.

"Oh, no!" cried Chris. "I know what that must be."

"What is it then?" asked Debbie.

"I left our trash bag outside. Now a raccoon has gotten into it," said Steve.

"What a mess that will be!" exclaimed Debbie.

Name_____ Date_____

Adjectives

Read the following sentences. Circle each adjective and underline the noun that adjective describes. Then write the adjectives with the nouns they describe on the lines below.

1. The (happy) child sang a (funny) song.

2. My (new) shoes hurt (my) feet.

3. A (beautiful) rainbow appeared in the (bright, blue) sky.

4. Tiffany found a (sad, wet) puppy.

5. (Loud) music played over (several) speakers.

6. (Eight)(oatmeal) cookies were left in the jar.

7. Matthew found his (long, lost) skateboard.

8. We went to a (scary) movie yesterday.

___happy—child___   ___funny—song___

___new—shoes___   ___my—feet___

___beautiful—rainbow___   ___bright, blue—sky___

___sad, wet—puppy___   ___loud—music___

___several—speakers___   ___eight, oatmeal—cookies___

___long, lost—skateboard___   ___scary—movie___

UNIT 3 Imagination • **Lesson 1** *Through Grandpa's Eyes*

Adjectives

Read the following sentences. Circle each adjective and underline the noun that adjective describes. Then write the adjectives with the nouns they describe on the lines below.

1. (Many) birds flew out of the (oak) tree.

2. Mike had (two) scoops of (chocolate) ice cream.

3. Diego and Kris like (pepperoni) pizza.

4. (Adventure) stories are (my) favorites.

5. We used (yellow) and (green) paint on the (tall) walls.

6. Is there (enough) cake for (eight) people?

7. There are a (dozen) (red) roses on the bush.

many—birds	oak—tree
two—scoops	chocolate—ice cream
pepperoni—pizza	Adventure—stories
my—favorites	yellow, green—paint
tall—walls	enough—cake
eight—people	dozen, red—roses

Adjectives

Improve the sentences below by adding adjectives. Rewrite the sentences on the lines that follow.

Tracy and Ana were friends. They read books together and told stories to each other. Sometimes they made up their own stories. Other times they would go to the park. The girls would run and play on the swing set and slides.

__Answers will vary. Sample responses appear__

__below.__

__Tracy and Ana were best friends. They read__

__many books together and told funny stories to__

__each other. Sometimes they made up their own__

__make-believe stories. Other times they would go__

__to the city park. The girls would run and play on__

__the tall swing set and long slides.__

_____

_____

_____

_____

_____

Name_____ Date_____

Contractions

Read the following sentences and circle the words that can be made into contractions. Write the contraction over the circle. Then copy the sentences, using the contractions, on the lines below.

1. My mother doesn't (does not) like mice!

   My mother doesn't like mice!

2. You've (You have) beautiful blue eyes.

   You've beautiful blue eyes.

3. I thought she'd (she had) lost her new coat.

   I thought she'd lost her new coat.

4. Molly can't (cannot) do division as well as I.

   Molly can't do division as well as I.

5. I think I'll (I will) try to go to sleep now.

   I think I'll try to go to sleep now.

6. We're (We are) going out to dinner tonight.

   We're going out to dinner tonight.

7. Who's (Who is) ringing that bell?

   Who's ringing that bell?

8. They're (They are) in the living room.

   They're in the living room.

UNIT 3 Imagination • **Lesson 2** *The Cat Who Became a Poet*

Contractions

Read the following sentences and circle the words that can be made into contractions. Write the contraction over the circle. Then copy the sentences, using the contractions, on the lines below.

1. Roy and Kitty (will not) eat broccoli.
   won't

   Roy and Kitty won't eat broccoli.

2. The classroom (does not) have a sink.
   doesn't

   The classroom doesn't have a sink.

3. (I am) sorry I forgot to call you.
   I'm

   I'm sorry I forgot to call you.

4. (They will) be home by 10:00.
   They'll

   They'll be home by 10:00.

5. Vince thought (he would) be good at tennis.
   he'd

   Vince thought he'd be good at tennis.

6. (We have) never visited Mexico.
   We've

   We've never visited Mexico.

7. The huge table (would not) fit in the doorway.
   wouldn't

   The huge table wouldn't fit in the doorway.

8. Dale (has not) finished his report on dragons.
   hasn't

   Dale hasn't finished his report on dragons.

UNIT 3 Imagination • **Lesson 2** *The Cat Who Became a Poet*

Contractions

Circle the errors in the following sentences. Then write the sentences correctly on the lines below.

1. I (dont) like cherry pie.

   I don't like cherry pie. _____

2. (Whose) singing in the hallway?

   Who's singing in the hallway? _____

3. Why (dont) you go tonight?

   Why don't you go tonight? _____

4. (Theirs) no one in the garden.

   There's no one in the garden. _____

5. We (couldnt) see who was home.

   We couldn't see who was home. _____

6. (Theyve) been very busy in class today.

   They've been very busy in class today. _____

7. She (wont) go to see scary movies.

   She won't go to see scary movies. _____

8. The puppy (wasnt) afraid of the water.

   The puppy wasn't afraid of the water. _____

UNIT 3 Imagination • **Lesson 3** *A Cloak for the Dreamer*

Verb Tenses

Read the story and circle each incorrect verb. Write the correct verb above the circle. Then write the story correctly on the lines below.

      Last week Harry (sees) [saw] some birds. The birds (are) [were] blue with tan chests. Harry (will) [did] not know what they were. The next day, Harry (looks) [looked] in his bird book. He found a picture of the birds. He (is) [was] excited. They (will be) [were] blue birds. He (learns) [learned] that blue birds are rare. Now Harry (looked) [looks] for birds each day. He hopes he will (saw) [see] another rare bird soon. Each day Harry (wrote) [writes] down the kinds of birds he sees.

    Last week Harry saw some birds. The birds were blue with tan chests. Harry did not know what they were. The next day Harry looked in his bird book. He found a picture of the birds. He was excited. They were blue birds. He learned that blue birds are rare. Now Harry looks for birds each day. He hopes he will see another rare bird soon. Each day Harry writes down the kinds of birds he sees.

Verb Tenses

Read the story and circle each incorrect verb. Write the correct verb above the circle. Then write the story correctly on the lines below.

Last week, Ellen ~~goes~~ **went** fishing with her dad. They ~~gets~~ **got** up very early. They ~~drives~~ **drove** to Bear Lake. Ellen ~~will hope~~ **hoped** to catch a big fish. She ~~tries~~ **tried** and ~~tries~~ **tried.** She ~~does~~ **did** not get a big one that day. She and Dad had a lot of fun anyway.

Next week, Ellen and Dad will ~~visited~~ **visit** the zoo. She ~~wanted~~ **wants** to see lions and bears. Dad says they will ~~saw~~ **see** many animals. Ellen ~~liked~~ **likes** to go places with Dad. She wonders what they will ~~did~~ **do** next.

____Last week, Ellen went fishing with her dad.____

____They got up very early. They drove to Bear Lake.____

____Ellen hoped to catch a big fish. She tried and____

____tried. She did not get a big one that day. She and____

____Dad had a lot of fun anyway.____

____Next week, Ellen and Dad will visit the zoo. She____

____wants to see lions and bears. Dad says they will____

____see many animals. Ellen likes to go places with____

____Dad. She wonders what they will do next.____

UNIT 3   Imagination • **Lesson 3** *A Cloak for the Dreamer*

Verb Tenses

Read the story and circle each incorrect verb. Write the correct verb above the circle. Then write the story correctly on the lines below.

    Yesterday, Jordan and his older brother (make) *made* dinner for their Mother. It (is) *was* her birthday. They (look) *looked* in her favorite cookbook to (picked) *pick* out a recipe. They (decide) *decided* to make pasta with sauce. They (wash) *washed* and cut up tomatoes, onions, and mushrooms and (cook) *cooked* them with spices. It (will smell) *smelled* delicious. Then they (boil) *boiled* the pasta. Mom (will be) *was* so happy when she saw what they (are) *were* making. Next month, Jordan (helped) *will help* his brother make a present for their Dad's birthday.

____Yesterday, Jordan and his older brother made____

dinner for their Mother. It was her birthday. They

looked in her favorite cookbook to pick out a

recipe. They decided to make pasta with sauce.

They washed and cut up tomatoes, onions, and

mushrooms and cooked them with spices. It

smelled delicious. Then they boiled the pasta.

Mom was so happy when she saw what they

were making. Next month, Jordan will help his

brother make a present for their Dad's birthday.

UNIT 3   Imagination • **Lesson 4** *Picasso*

Plural Nouns

Read the following sentences and circle the nouns that should be plural. Write the correct plural noun over the circle. Then copy the sentences correctly on the lines below.

1. My best friend has four (dog.) *dogs*

   My best friend has four dogs.

2. I need to ride on two different (bus) to get home. *buses*

   I need to ride on two different buses to get home.

3. The (leaf) were falling off the tree. *leaves*

   The leaves were falling off the tree.

4. The orchestra had three (piano.) *pianos*

   The orchestra had three pianos.

5. Many (woman) were in the choir. *women*

   Many women were in the choir.

6. Are there many (candy) in the jar? *candies*

   Are there many candies in the jar?

Plural Nouns

Read the following sentences and circle the nouns that should be plural. Write the correct plural noun over the circle. Then copy the sentences correctly on the lines below.

1. I will need three (copy) of your report.
   copies

   I will need three copies of your report.

2. Before I go to bed, I must brush my (tooth.)
   teeth

   Before I go to bed, I must brush my teeth.

3. Mandy and Jill like to ride their (bike.)
   bikes

   Mandy and Jill like to ride their bikes.

4. The hungry (child) waited for their dinners.
   children

   The hungry children waited for their dinners.

5. Many (man) like to watch football.
   men

   Many men like to watch football.

6. Were you throwing (stick) for your dogs to fetch?
   sticks

   Were you throwing sticks for your dogs to fetch?

UNIT 3 Imagination • **Lesson 4** *Picasso*

Plural Nouns

Read the following sentences and circle the nouns that should be plural. Write the correct plural noun over the circle. Then copy the sentences correctly on the lines below.

1. Our classroom needs more (bookshelfs.)
   bookshelves

   Our classroom needs more bookshelves._____

2. Place the (boxs) in the corner.
   boxes

   Place the boxes in the corner._____

3. Did you see those (deers) cross the trail?
   deer

   Did you see those deer cross the trail?_____

4. The (gooses) flew overhead.
   geese

   The geese flew overhead._____

5. The (childs) were told to be careful and to not get hurt.
   children

   The children were told to be careful to not

   get hurt._____

6. The (mans) finished the barn in one weekend.
   men

   The men finished the barn in one weekend._____

Articles

Read the following sentences and circle the correct articles.
Then copy the sentences correctly on the lines below.

1. Do you have (a)/an pet?

   Do you have a pet?

2. Mom put a/(an) apple in my lunch.

   Mom put an apple in my lunch.

3. (The)/A first person to the finish line wins!

   The first person to the finish line wins!

4. Maria told a/(an) impossible tale.

   Maria told an impossible tale.

5. (The)/A last scene in the movie was my favorite.

   The last scene in the movie was my favorite.

6. A/(An) old man carried (a)/an cane.

   An old man carried a cane.

7. The/(A) bunch of birds flew across the sky.

   A bunch of birds flew across the sky.

8. My aunt has (a)/an fluffy rabbit.

   My aunt has a fluffy rabbit.

UNIT 3 Imagination • **Lesson 5** *The Emperor's New Clothes*

Articles

**Read the following sentences and circle the correct articles.
Then copy the sentences correctly on the lines below.**

1. The/A cute little kitten has a/an long tail.

   The cute little kitten has a long tail.

2. A/An angry bumblebee can be scary.

   An angry bumblebee can be scary.

3. We drove to the/a nearest restaurant for dinner.

   We drove to the nearest restaurant for dinner.

4. Everyone likes to read the/a good book.

   Everyone likes to read a good book.

5. Baseball is a/an all American sport.

   Baseball is an all American sport.

6. The/A wounded wolf howled in pain.

   The wounded wolf howled in pain.

7. Max is a/an Englishman and a/an gentleman.

   Max is an Englishman and a gentleman.

8. Do you eat a/the bowl of ice cream every night?

   Do you eat a bowl of ice cream every night?

UNIT 3   Imagination • **Lesson 5** *The Emperor's New Clothes*

Articles

Read the following sentences and circle the incorrect articles.
Then copy the sentences correctly on the lines below.

Lydia read her little brother (the) story. It was about (the) little dog and (the) kitten. At first, they had (an) hard time getting along. Then they helped each other solve (the) problem. After that, they understood each other and always had (an) good time together.

Lydia read her little brother a story. It was about
a little dog and a kitten. At first, they had a hard
time getting along. Then they helped each other
solve a problem. After that, they understood each
other and always had a good time together.

_____

_____

_____

_____

_____

_____

_____

UNIT 3 Imagination • **Lesson 6** *Roxaboxen*

Adjectives and Adverbs

Read the story and circle the adjectives. Then underline the adverbs. Write each adjective and adverb under the correct heading on the lines below.

Insects can live in (many) places. Some live in (freezing) snow. Others live in (burning) deserts. There are insects in the (steamy) (rain) forests. Insects can live in streams where water runs <u>swiftly</u>. If you look <u>carefully</u>, you may find insects buried in (old) books. Insects can be found by the (salty) ocean. There they live in the (wet) sand. They dig holes where the waves <u>quickly</u> flow.

Adjectives	**Adverbs**
many	swiftly
freezing	carefully
burning	quickly
steamy	
rain	
old	
salty	
wet	

UNIT 3 Imagination • **Lesson 6** *Roxaboxen*

Adjectives and Adverbs

Read the story and circle the adjectives. Then underline the adverbs. Write each adjective and adverb under the correct heading on the lines below.

Jay ran quickly to the mailbox. He opened the little door. He found three letters for Dad, a new magazine for Mom, and a beautiful postcard. The picture postcard was for Jay. His Aunt Kate had carefully printed his name and address. She usually sent pretty cards or funny letters. Jay kept the cards and letters safely tucked away in a box.

Adjectives	Adverbs
little	quickly
three	carefully
new	usually
beautiful	safely
picture	
pretty	
funny	

UNIT 3 Imagination • **Lesson 6** *Roxaboxen*

Adjectives and Adverbs

Read the story and circle the adjectives. Then underline the adverbs. Write each adjective and adverb under the correct heading on the lines below.

Marissa likes to draw and paint (beautiful) pictures. Sometimes she uses (real) places and things for her models. Other times she uses her (own) (active) imagination. She uses colors <u>well</u>. She prefers (bright) colors. So when the sun is shining <u>brightly</u>, she <u>happily</u> goes <u>outside</u> to look for (interesting) things to draw or paint.

Adjectives	Adverbs
beautiful	well
real	brightly
own	happily
active	outside
bright	
interesting	

UNIT 4 Money • **Lesson I** *A New Coat for Anna*

Prepositions and Prepositional Phrases

Read each of the following sentences and underline the prepositional phrase. Circle the preposition in each prepositional phrase. Then copy the prepositional phrases on the lines below.

1. Janice wiped (off) the dishes.

2. We walked slowly (toward) the bridge.

3. (After) the movie, they went for ice cream.

4. Jake parked his bike (near) my door.

5. Everyone (in) the classroom liked art.

6. (During) the tornado, we hid (in) the cellar.

7. Rachel tied a bow (around) her hair.

8. We will travel (to) New Mexico.

9. All the children (on) the playground were cold.

10. (From) the sky, the rain poured down.

off the dishes	toward the bridge
After the movie	near my door
in the classroom	During the tornado
in the cellar	around her hair
to New Mexico	on the playground
from the sky	

Name_____ Date_____

Prepositions and Prepositional Phrases

Read each of the following sentences and underline the prepositional phrase. Circle the preposition in each prepositional phrase. Then copy the prepositional phrases on the lines below.

1. The toddler colored (outside) the lines.

2. Marc lives (past) the river.

3. (Before) sunrise, we left (for) our fishing trip.

4. Liz climbed quickly (through) the tunnel.

5. Josh ate all his dinner (except) his green beans.

6. Kyle walked (beside) Miles and (behind) Jessica.

7. (At) exactly 12:00, the bell rang.

8. (Since) this morning, it has not stopped raining.

9. Faith jumped (onto) the trampoline.

10. I swung (at) the ball and ran (to) first base.

outside the lines   past the river

Before sunrise   for our fishing trip

through the tunnel   except his green beans

besides Miles   behind Jessica

At exactly 12:00   Since this morning

onto the trampoline   at the ball

to first base

UNIT 4 Money • **Lesson 1** *A New Coat for Anna*

Prepositions and Prepositional Phrases

Read each of the following sentences and underline the prepositional phrase. Circle the preposition in each prepositional phrase. Then copy the prepositional phrases on the lines below.

1. Wash the apples (in) the sink.

2. Nathan carried the bag (to) the car.

3. The cat played (with) the string.

4. The train rolled (down) the track.

5. Smoke disappeared (into) the sky.

6. The children lined up (at) the door.

7. Nina congratulated herself (after) the test.

8. Thomas slid (into) home base.

9. Melinda washed her hands (before) dinner.

10. Carlos worked hard (on) his homework.

in the sink	to the car
with the string	down the track
into the sky	at the door
after the test	into home base
before dinner	on his homework

UNIT 4   Money • **Lesson 2** *Alexander, Who Used to Be Rich Last Sunday*

Subjects and Predicates

Read the following sentences. Circle the subject in each sentence. Underline the predicate in each sentence.

1. My (mother) went to the store.

2. (Keith) wrote a funny story.

3. (Matt) and his (dog) hiked up the hill.

4. (They) loved going to concerts.

5. (Paula) plays the violin very well.

6. At 7:00, (Dad) left for work.

7. The small (child) cried for his mother.

8. (Ben) and (Riley) are best friends.

On the lines below write three of your own sentences, circling the subjects and underlining the predicates.

1. Answers will vary _____

_____

2. Answers will vary _____

_____

3. Answers will vary _____

_____

UNIT 4 Money • **Lesson 2** *Alexander, Who Used to Be Rich Last Sunday*

Subjects and Predicates

Read the following sentences. Circle the subject in each sentence. Underline the predicate in each sentence.

1. The (dog) growled at the stranger.

2. (Marsha) found my lost charm bracelet.

3. Until yesterday, (I) thought that I couldn't ride a bike.

4. (Ali) and (Jill) play basketball.

5. Our (friends) live on Market Street.

6. A small (hummingbird) sips from the feeder.

7. My (sister) gave me a special gift.

8. (Jackie) and her (mother) look very much alike.

On the lines below write three of your own sentences, circling the subjects and underlining the predicates.

1. Answers will vary _____

   _____

2. Answers will vary _____

   _____

3. Answers will vary _____

   _____

UNIT 4   Money • **Lesson 2** *Alexander, Who Used to Be Rich Last Sunday*

Subjects and Predicates

Read the following sentences. Circle the subject in each complete sentence. Underline the predicate in each complete sentence. Complete the incomplete sentences by adding either a subject or predicate.

1. (Jan) and (Maria) are baking a cake.

2. (We) found a puppy.

3. The (cat) climbed a tree.

4. (Martin) is reading a book.

5. Nicholas __Answers will vary.__ .

6. __Answers will vary.__ are taking a train to Denver.

7. __Answers will vary.__ went to a movie yesterday.

8. Either Jason or Ted __Answers will vary.__ .

On the lines below write three of your own sentences, circling the subjects and underlining the predicates.

1. __Answers will vary_____

_____

2. __Answers will vary_____

_____

3. __Answers will vary_____

_____

UNIT 4 Money • **Lesson 3** *Kids Did It! in Business*

Periods in Abbreviations, Titles, and Initials

Read the following story. Indicate with an arrow each place where there should be a period. Then copy the story correctly on the lines below.

Mr James H Buckland makes wooden chairs. He shares a workshop with Dr Angela L Jones, who makes tables. Their workshop is on 41st St They are going to sell their tables and chairs at the fair on Saturday. Their booth is located on Columbus Blvd Other booths are located on Oak Ave Mr Buckland and Dr Jones hope to sell enough tables and chairs to buy wood for next year's fair.

Mr. James H. Buckland makes wooden chairs. He shares a workshop with Dr. Angela L. Jones, who makes tables. Their workshop is on 41st St. They are going to sell their tables and chairs at the fair on Saturday. Their booth is located on Columbus Blvd. Other booths are located on Oak Ave. Mr. Buckland and Dr. Jones hope to sell enough tables and chairs to buy wood for next year's fair.

_____

UNIT 4 Money • **Lesson 3** *Kids Did It! in Business*

Periods in Abbreviations, Titles, and Initials

Read the following story. Indicate with an arrow each place where there should be a period. Then copy the story correctly on the lines below.

Mr and Mrs Frank J Johnson and their dog, Buster, were lost! They were trying to find the office of Buster's veterinarian, Dr Mindy K McNight. It seemed like they were driving around in circles. They turned left on Pacific Ave and right on Magnolia St

"Arf, arf," barked Buster as they finally found Dr McNight's office on the corner of Maple Blvd and Magnolia St

Mr. and Mrs. Frank J. Johnson and their dog,

Buster, were lost! They were trying to find the

office of Buster's veterinarian, Dr. Mindy K.

McNight. It seemed like they were driving around

in circles. They turned left on Pacific Ave. and

right on Magnolia St.

"Arf, arf," barked Buster as they finally found

Dr. McNight's office on the corner of Maple Blvd.

and Magnolia St.

_____

UNIT 4 Money • **Lesson 3** *Kids Did It! in Business*

Periods in Abbreviations, Titles, and Initials

Read the following sentences. Indicate with an arrow each place where there should be a period. Write a period over each arrow. Then copy the sentences correctly on the lines below.

1. Dr Wilson is our family doctor.

   <u>**Dr. Wilson is our family doctor.**</u>

2. His office is on Mayfair Ave.

   <u>**His office is on Mayfair Ave.**</u>

3. My full name is Martin H Ramirez.

   <u>**My full name is Martin H. Ramirez.**</u>

4. Mrs Hamilton is the school librarian.

   <u>**Mrs. Hamilton is the school librarian.**</u>

5. Gen Simms and his family live next door.

   <u>**Gen. Simms and his family live next door.**</u>

6. Do you live on Maple St?

   <u>**Do you live on Maple St.?**</u>

UNIT 4 Money • **Lesson 4** *The Cobbler's Song*

Possessive Pronouns

Read the following sentences. Fill in the blanks with the possessive pronoun suggested by the words in parentheses. Then copy the sentences using the correct possessive pronouns on the lines below.

1. ____My____ room can be very messy. (The room belonging to me.)

   My room can be very messy._____

2. Did you see ___their___ lost dog? (The dog belonging to them.)

   Did you see their lost dog?_____

3. The drawing is ___his___. (The drawing belonging to him.)

   The drawing is his._____

4. Suzy dropped ___her___ book. (The book belonging to Suzy.)

   Suzy dropped her book._____

5. That new car is ___ours___. (The car belonging to us.)

   That new car is ours._____

6. I believe that CD is ___mine___. (The CD belonging to me.)

   I believe that CD is mine._____

7. ___Your___ turn will be coming up soon. (The turn belonging to you.)

   Your turn will be coming up soon._____

8. The school has ___its___ own science lab. (The science lab belonging to the school.)

   The school has its own science lab._____

UNIT 4 Money • **Lesson 4** *The Cobbler's Song*

Possessive Pronouns

Read the following sentences. Fill in the blanks with the possessive pronoun suggested by the words in parentheses. Then copy the sentences using the correct possessive pronouns on the lines below.

1. Karen broke ____her____ leg while skiing. (The leg belonging to Karen.)

   Karen broke her leg while skiing._____

2. All of the bikes were ___theirs__. (The bikes belonging to them.)

   All of the bikes were theirs._____

3. The store likes to hire ____its____ own accountants. (Accountants belonging to the store.)

   The store likes to hire its own accountants._____

4. The old man likes ____his____ apples very ripe. (Apples belonging to the old man.)

   The old man likes his apples very ripe._____

5. The sweet smelling lotion is ___mine__. (Lotion belonging to me.)

   The sweet smelling lotion is mine._____

6. The soccer trophy is ___ours___. (The trophy belonging to us.)

   The soccer trophy is ours._____

7. ___Your___ friend is very nice. (The friend belonging to you.)

   Your friend is very nice._____

8. ___My___ shoes are on the wrong feet! (The shoes belonging to me.)

   My shoes are on the wrong feet!_____

Name_____ Date _____

Possessive Pronouns

Read the following sentences. Fill in the blanks with the possessive pronoun suggested by the words in parentheses. Then copy the sentences using the correct possessive pronouns on the lines below.

1. The kitten has lost ____its____ toy. (the toy belonging to the kitten)

   <u>The kitten has lost its toy.</u>

2. ____Your____ drawing is very good. (the drawing belonging to you)

   <u>Your drawing is very good.</u>

3. Michael forgot ____his____ homework. (the homework belonging to Michael)

   <u>Michael forgot his homework.</u>

4. Lupita showed ____her____ good grades to ____her____ parents. (the grades belonging to Lupita; the parents belonging to Lupita)

   <u>Lupita showed her good grades to her</u>

   <u>parents.</u>

5. ____Our____ neighbors invited us to ____their____ house for a barbecue. (the neighbors belonging to us; the house belonging to them)

   <u>Our neighbors invited us to their house for a</u>

   <u>barbecue.</u>

6. The dog in that yard is ____theirs____. (the dog belonging to them)

   <u>The dog in that yard is theirs.</u>

UNIT 4 Money • **Lesson 5** *Four Dollars and Fifty Cents*

Subject-Verb Agreement

Read the story and circle each incorrect verb. Write the correct verb over each circle. Then write the story correctly on the lines below.

　　　　　　　　　　　　　　live　　　　　　　　　　　　　dig
　　Ants are interesting. Hundreds of ants (lives) together. The ants (digs)
　　　　　　　　　　　connect
tunnels in the ground. The tunnels (connects) to many rooms as well as
　　　　　　　　　　work　　　　　　　　　　keep
other tunnels. The ants (works) hard. Some ants (keeps) the tunnels open.
　　　　　　　　　　　　　　　　　　　protect
Some take care of baby ants. Other ants (protects) the nest. You often
see　　　　　　　　　　　　　　　　find
(sees) ants on the sidewalk. These ants (finds) food for all the other ants.

　　__Ants are interesting. Hundreds of ants live__

__together. The ants dig tunnels in the ground. The__

__tunnels connect to many rooms as well as other__

__tunnels. The ants work hard. Some ants keep__

__the tunnels open. Some take care of baby ants.__

__Other ants protect the nest. You often see ants__

__on the sidewalk. These ants find food for all the__

__other ants.__

_____

_____

_____

UNIT 4 Money • **Lesson 5** *Four Dollars and Fifty Cents*

Subject-Verb Agreement

Read the story and circle each incorrect verb. Write the correct verb over each circle. Then write the story correctly on the lines below.

      Mom and I ~~lives~~ *live* in the city. We don't ~~has~~ *have* a yard. Mom got a big pot and filled it with dirt. We ~~puts~~ *put* plants in the dirt and watered them every day. Mom and I ~~takes~~ *take* good care of our plants. Now the plants ~~has~~ *have* beautiful flowers on them. Mom and I ~~hopes~~ *hope* that someday we will ~~has~~ *have* more plants to grow. The plants ~~seems~~ *seem* to know that they are loved.

    Mom and I live in the city. We don't have a yard. Mom got a big pot and filled it with dirt. We put plants in the dirt and watered them every day. Mom and I take good care of our plants. Now the plants have beautiful flowers on them. Mom and I hope that someday we will have more plants to grow. The plants seem to know that they are loved.

UNIT 4   Money • **Lesson 5** *Four Dollars and Fifty Cents*

Subject-Verb Agreement

Read the story and circle each incorrect verb. Write the correct verb over each circle. Then write the story correctly on the lines below.

My parents and I (likes) to hear music. Sometimes we (goes) to
like   go

symphony concerts downtown. The symphony plays classical

music. Since we have started going, I (has) learned a lot about music.
have

My neighbor (have) also taught me about classical music. He is a
has

musician in the symphony. He (play) violin. I (hopes) to take lessons from
plays   hope

him some day.

_____My parents and I like to hear music._____

_____Sometimes we go to symphony concerts_____

_____downtown. The symphony plays classical music._____

_____Since we have started going, I have learned a lot_____

_____about music. My neighbor has also taught me_____

_____about classical music. He is a musician in the_____

_____symphony. He plays violin. I hope to take lessons_____

_____from him some day._____

_____

_____

UNIT 4 Money • **Lesson 6** *The Go-Around Dollar*

Adverbs

Read the sentences below and circle the adverbs. Draw a line under each verb that an adverb tells about. Then write the adverbs and the words they tell about on the lines below.

1. The dog barked loudly.

   loudly—barked

2. The snow completely covered the bushes.

   completely—covered

3. Marty touches the keyboard lightly.

   lightly—touches

4. The car stopped instantly.

   instantly—stopped

5. The truck nearly crashed.

   nearly—crashed

6. Misty smiled happily at me.

   happily—smiled

7. The stars shone brightly in the night.

   brightly—shone

8. Lisa looks shyly at Ms. Beck.

   shyly—looks

Adverbs

Read the sentences below and circle the adverbs. Draw a line under each verb that an adverb tells about. Then write the adverbs and the words they tell about on the lines below.

1. The snail <u>crawls</u> (slowly) across the lawn.

   slowly—crawls

2. Mom <u>clapped</u> (loudly) after the play.

   loudly—clapped

3. The choir <u>sings</u> (joyously.)

   joyously—sings

4. I was (hopelessly) <u>confused</u> on the test.

   hopelessly—confused

5. Dad <u>paints</u> (well.)

   well—paints

6. The birds (constantly) <u>chirped</u>.

   constantly—chirped

7. I (carefully) <u>watched</u> my piano teacher.

   carefully—watched

8. Jordan <u>draws</u> (beautifully.)

   beautifully—draws

UNIT 4 Money • **Lesson 6** *The Go-Around Dollar*

Adverbs

Read the sentences below and circle the adverbs. Draw a line under each verb that an adverb tells about. Then write the adverbs and the words they tell about on the lines below.

1. The train rolled (forcefully) down the track.

   forcefully—rolled_____

2. The dogs ran (wildly) in the yard.

   wildly—ran_____

3. Fernando (never) forgets his sister's birthday.

   never—forgets_____

4. I (hardly) slept last night.

   hardly—slept_____

5. Theresa worked (quickly) on her project.

   quickly—worked_____

6. Spring arrived (early.)

   early—arrived_____

7. Evening traffic moved (along) (slowly.)

   slowly, along—moved_____

8. The candle burned (faintly) in the window.

   faintly—burned_____

Name_____ Date_____

Subject-Verb Agreement

Read the story and circle each incorrect verb. Write the correct verb over each circle. Then write the story correctly on the lines below.

is   eats   does
Ken (are) in a hurry today. He (eat) his breakfast fast. He (do) not want
wants   are
to be late. He (want) to sit by Paco on the bus. They (is) good friends. Paco
are   want
and Ken (is) making a poster for the school fair. They (wants) to plan the
             hope
poster before school. Then, they can work on it at recess. They (hopes) to
    is
finish the poster today. It (are) going to look great.

Ken is in a hurry today. He eats his breakfast
fast. He does not want to be late. He wants to sit
by Paco on the bus. They are good friends. Paco
and Ken are making a poster for the school fair.
They want to plan the poster before school. Then,
they can work on it at recess. They hope to finish
the poster today. It is going to look great.

_____

_____

_____

UNIT 4   Money • **Lesson 7** *Uncle Jed's Barbershop*

Subject-Verb Agreement

Read the story and circle each incorrect verb. Write the correct verb over each circle. Then write the story correctly on the lines below.

    On rainy days, Sally and I (likes) to visit Grandma. She lets us play
        like

with her jewelry boxes. She (have) fancy pins she (call) brooches. She (have)
            has   *calls*   *has*

pretty necklaces and bracelets, too. We (loves) to put on her old dresses
                         love

and sparkly jewelry. We (thinks) we look lovely. Grandma (call) us her
          think   *calls*

princesses. She (take) our pictures. We all (shares) a happy tea party.
          takes   *share*

Someday, we will giggle at the silly pictures.

     On rainy days, Sally and I like to visit Grandma.
She lets us play with her jewelry boxes. She has
fancy pins she calls brooches. She has pretty
necklaces and bracelets, too. We love to put on
her old dresses and sparkly jewelry. We think we
look lovely. Grandma calls us her princesses. She
takes our pictures. We all share a happy tea
party. Someday, we will giggle at the silly
pictures.

UNIT 4 Money • **Lesson 7** *Uncle Jed's Barbershop*

Subject-Verb Agreement

Read the story and circle each incorrect verb. Write the correct verb over each circle. Then write the story correctly on the lines below.

                          want   **tell**
Sarita and Mario (wants) a puppy. Their parents (tells) them it is a lot of
           visit   **stay**
work. They (visits) their cousin who has a dog. They (stays) for the whole
                                       put
weekend to help take care of the dog. They (puts) out food and water for
                                              take
the dog in the morning and at night. They play with the dog. They (takes)
him on a walk. They come back after a movie to let the dog outside.
                        want
Sarita and Mario still (wants) a puppy even though it is a lot of work.

    Sarita and Mario want a puppy. Their parents
tell them it is a lot of work. They visit their cousin
who has a dog. They stay for the whole weekend
to help take care of the dog. They put out food
and water for the dog in the morning and at
night. They play with the dog. They take him on a
walk. They come back after a movie to let the
dog outside. Sarita and Mario still want a puppy
even though it is a lot of work.

UNIT 5 Storytelling • **Lesson I** *A Story A Story*

Sentence Structure-Simple and Compound

Read the following pairs of simple sentences. Insert a comma and a conjunction where they belong to combine the two sentences. Write the conjunction you would use above the comma. Then write the new compound sentences on the lines below.

1. Mom baked a cake, **and** We ate it immediately.

   Mom baked a cake, and we ate it immediately.

2. I like oranges, **but** I love grapes.

   I like oranges, but I love grapes.

3. Did you make those cookies? **or** Did you buy them?

   Did you make those cookies, or did you buy them?

4. I like to play tennis, **and** I have a new racket.

   I like to play tennis, and I have a new racket.

5. Do you like root beer? **or** Would you rather have ginger ale?

   Do you like root beer, or would you rather have ginger ale?

6. There were many apples on the tree, **and** We picked all of them.

   There were many apples on the tree, and we picked all of them.

Sentence Structure-Simple and Compound

Read the following pairs of simple sentences. Insert a comma and a conjunction where they belong to combine the two sentences. Write the conjunction you would use above the comma. Then write the new compound sentences on the lines below.

1. The waitress brought our lunch, _{and} We all enjoyed it.

   The waitress brought our lunch, and we all
   enjoyed it.

2. We looked everywhere for our keys, _{but} We couldn't find them.

   We looked everywhere for our keys, but we
   couldn't find them.

3. Mona slid down the slide, _{and} She played on the jungle gym.

   Mona slid down the slide, and she played on
   the jungle gym.

4. Can you come to my house? _{or} Should I come to your house?

   Can you come to my house, or should I come
   to your house?

5. Rob finished the race, _{but} He didn't win.

   Rob finished the race, but he didn't win.

UNIT 5 Storytelling • **Lesson I** *A Story A Story*

Sentence Structure—Simple and Compound

Read the following pairs of simple sentences. Insert a comma and a conjunction where they belong to combine the two sentences. Write the conjunction you would use above the comma. Then write the new compound sentences on the lines below.

1. The wind started to howl, *and* The waves began to rock.

   <u>The wind started to howl, and the waves began to rock.</u>

2. Would you like to have a picnic? *or* Would you like to go to the zoo?

   <u>Would you like to have a picnic, or would you like to go to the zoo?</u>

3. Angel made a poster for the party, *and* Hector made cookies.

   <u>Angel made a poster for the party, and Hector made cookies.</u>

4. Jenna wants a cake, *but* Cassie prefers cookies.

   <u>Jenna wants a cake, but Cassie prefers cookies.</u>

5. Trevor hit the ball far, *and* Chris ran to home plate.

   <u>Trevor hit the ball far, and Chris ran to home plate.</u>

6. Do you want to ride bikes? *or* Do you prefer walking?

   <u>Do you want to ride bikes, or do you prefer walking?</u>

UNIT 5 Storytelling • **Lesson 2** *Oral History*

Colons

Read the letter. Look for places where colons should go and mark them with arrows. Then copy the letter correctly on the lines below.

To the Scouts in Troop 17͙

    I am writing to remind you of the upcoming campout. We will leave on Saturday between 8͙30 and 9͙00 in the morning. Please be at my house no later than 8͙15. We should return on Sunday at about 7͙00 in the evening.

    The following scouts will be in charge of making dinner͙ Ben, Paco, Tony, and Bryce. Breakfast will be made by the following scouts͙ Paul, Jon, and Felix.

To the Scouts in Troop 17:

    I am writing to remind you of the upcoming campout. We will leave on Saturday between 8:30 and 9:00 in the morning. Please be at my house no later than 8:15. We should return on Sunday at about 7:00 in the evening.

    The following scouts will be in charge of making dinner: Ben, Paco, Tony, and Bryce. Breakfast will be made by the following scouts: Paul, Jon, and Felix.

UNIT 5 Storytelling • **Lesson 2** *Oral History*

Colons

Read the letter. Look for places where colons should go and mark them with arrows. Then copy the letter correctly on the lines below.

To the Ladies of the Garden Club ⌄

    This is to remind you of the next meeting on Tuesday, May 5th. As usual, the meeting will begin at 10⌄00 a.m. and end at 11⌄45 a.m. Lunch will then be served promptly at 12⌄00 p.m. The following ladies will be making our lunch ⌄ Mrs. Keel, Ms. Hardy, and Mrs. Farr.

Sincerely,
Miss Marshall

To the Ladies of the Garden Club:

    This is to remind you of the next meeting on Tuesday, May 5th. As usual, the meeting will begin at 10:00 a.m. and end at 11:45 a.m. Lunch will then be served promptly at 12:00 p.m. The following ladies will be making our lunch: Mrs. Keel, Ms. Hardy, and Mrs. Farr.

Sincerely,
Miss Marshall

Colons

Read the letter. Look for places where colons should go and mark them with arrows. Then copy the letter correctly on the lines below.

To Ms. Melanie Sutton

    Thank you for agreeing to meet with our class for Career Day. Career Day will take place on May 30th. Presentations will occur between 12 00 p.m. and 3 00 p.m.

    For the presentation, we have the following items available for your use overhead projector, audiotape player, videotape player, and a computer with Internet access.

               Sincerely,

               Ms. Polermo

To Ms. Melanie Sutton:

   Thank you for agreeing to meet with our class for Career Day. Career Day will take place on May 30th. Presentations will occur between 12:00 p.m. and 3:00 p.m.

   For the presentation, we have the following items available for your use: overhead projector, audiotape player, videotape player, and a computer with Internet access.

UNIT 5   Storytelling • **Lesson 3** *Storm in the Night*

Conjunctions

Read the following sentences and circle the conjunction that fits best in each sentence. Then copy the sentences correctly on the lines below.

1. Jessica read the first chapter, (**and,** or, but) Samantha read the next chapter.

   Jessica read the first chapter, and Samantha read the next chapter.

2. Judy is a good friend, (and, or, **but**) Becky is my best friend.

   Judy is a good friend, but Becky is my best friend.

3. I could study now, (and, **or,** but) I could study after dinner.

   I could study now, or I could study after dinner.

4. Do you buy your lunch, (and, **or,** but) do you bring it from home?

   Do you buy your lunch, or do you bring it from home?

5. Tom loves football, (**and,** or, but) he also loves track.

   Tom loves football, and he also loves track.

6. Do you want a glass of water, (and, **or,** but) would you like some soda?

   Do you want a glass of water, or would you like some soda?

UNIT 5   **Storytelling • Lesson 3** *Storm in the Night*

Conjunctions

Read the following sentences and circle the conjunction that fits best in each sentence. Then copy the sentences correctly on the lines below.

1. Dave swims the backstroke, (and, or, but) he also swims freestyle.

   Dave swims the backstroke, and he also

   swims freestyle.

2. My sister is smart, (and, or, but) I am smarter.

   My sister is smart, but I am smarter.

3. My dog is very sweet, (and, or, but) she is gentle with children.

   My dog is very sweet, and she is gentle with

   children.

4. Can I drive you to school, (and, or, but) do you want to ride the bus?

   Can I drive you to school, or do you want to

   ride the bus?

5. Mrs. Snyder was talking, (and, or, but) no one was paying attention.

   Mrs. Snyder was talking, but no one was

   paying attention.

6. Will you help me, (and, or, but) should I ask for Mom's help?

   Will you help me, or should I ask for Mom's

   help?

Conjunctions

Put a comma and a conjunction where they are necessary to combine the two sentences next to each number. Write the conjunction you use above the comma. Then write the new compound sentences on the lines below.

but
1. Trains are fast, Planes are faster.

   Trains are fast, but planes are faster.

but
2. I like apples, Watermelon is my favorite fruit.

   I like apples, but watermelon is my favorite

   fruit.

and
3. Loren sang, Clark played the guitar.

   Loren sang, and Clark played the guitar.

or
4. Would you like to draw pictures? Do you prefer to paint?

   Would you like to draw pictures, or do you

   prefer to paint?

but
5. Aliya said she was fine, I thought she looked tired.

   Aliya said she was fine, but I thought she

   looked tired.

but
6. The party was in two days, Hector did not want to wait.

   The party was in two days, but Hector did not

   want to wait.

Name_____ Date _____

Capitalization—Titles

Read the following story and circle words that need to be capitalized. Then write the paragraph correctly on the lines below.

My little sister got a book for her birthday called (the children's) (book) of (nursery rhymes.) The first chapter, ("old favorites,") is the one I like best. It has all the poems I loved best when I was little: ("humpty-) (dumpty,") ("jack) and (jill,") and ("three blind mice.") Another chapter is ("new) (poems) for a (new age.") Those poems have titles like ("jump around) the (sky") and ("blue july.") I think I like the book as much as my sister!

My little sister got a book for her birthday
called The Children's Book of Nursery Rhymes.
The first chapter, "Old Favorites," is the one I like
best. It has all the poems I loved best when I was
little: "Humpty-Dumpty," "Jack and Jill," and
"Three Blind Mice." Another chapter is "New
Poems for a New Age." Those poems have titles
like "Jump Around the Sky" and "Blue July." I
think I like the book as much as my sister!

_____

UNIT 5 Storytelling • **Lesson 4** *Carving the Pole*

Capitalization—Titles

Read the following story and circle words that need to be capitalized. Then write the paragraphs correctly on the lines below.

Our teacher taught us how to write poems about the seasons. Bill's was called ("winter's snow.") Jesse wrote one called ("orange september") and another called ("spring time.")

We decided to make a poetry book. Our book has two chapters: ("sunshine") and ("snowfall.") Each chapter has many great poems, but we haven't picked a title for our book yet. Some of us want to call it (seasons) and others want to call it (times) of the (year.) What title do you like?

_____Our teacher taught us how to write poems_____

_____about the seasons. Bill's was called "Winter's_____

_____Snow." Jesse wrote one called "Orange_____

_____September" and another called "Spring Time."_____

_____We decided to make a poetry book. Our book_____

_____has two chapters: "Sunshine" and "Snowfall."_____

_____Each chapter has many great poems, but we_____

_____haven't picked a title for our book yet. Some of_____

_____us want to call it *Seasons* and others want to call_____

_____it *Times of the Year*. What title do you like?_____

Capitalization—Titles

Read the following story and circle words that need to be capitalized. Then write the paragraph correctly on the lines below.

Paco is writing a book. He is calling it (the things) I (see.) He has even written several chapters. One chapter is called ("playground sights.") Another is called ("scenes) in (my house.") He is working on a chapter called ("city sights.")He wants to write another called ("views change)with the Seasons."

    Paco is writing a book. He is calling it *The Things I See.* He has even written several chapters. One chapter is called "Playground Sights." Another is called "Scenes in My House." He is working on a chapter called "City Sights." He wants to write another called "Views Change with the Seasons."

UNIT 5   **Storytelling** • **Lesson 5** *The Keeping Quilt*

Capitalization—Proper Nouns

Read the story and circle each noun that should begin with a capital letter. Write the noun correctly above the circle. Then write the story correctly on the lines below.

    Russ had a card for the ⟨riverside⟩ Library. *Riverside* He likes to borrow books by Sam ⟨jones.⟩ *Jones* The books are about a boy named ⟨mike⟩ *Mike* Sims. Mike and his friends have a secret club. It is the Star ⟨detective⟩ *Detective* Club. They try to solve mysteries. The mysteries take place at ⟨grove⟩ *Grove* School. Russ has read every book about Mike ⟨sims.⟩ *Sims* He even wrote a letter to ⟨mr.⟩ *Mr.* Jones.

Russ asked him to write more books about Mike Sims.

    Russ had a card for the Riverside Library. He likes to borrow books by Sam Jones. The books are about a boy named Mike Sims. Mike and his friends have a secret club. It is the Star Detective Club. They try to solve mysteries. The mysteries take place at Grove School. Russ has read every book about Mike Sims. He even wrote a letter to Mr. Jones. Russ asked him to write more books about Mike Sims.

UNIT 5 Storytelling • **Lesson 5** *The Keeping Quilt*

Capitalization—Proper Nouns

Read the story and circle each noun that should begin with a capital letter. Write the noun correctly above the circle. Then write the story correctly on the lines below.

When (mrs.) Kerr was a girl she lived on a farm in (missouri.) One
spring day, she found a baby duck. Mrs. (kerr) named it (webster.) She kept
(webster) for a pet. (mrs. kerr) also had a dog named (wags.) Wags liked
(webster.) He let the duckling sit on his back. In the summer, (mrs. kerr.)
Webster, and (wags) went swimming at (blue) Lake. They must have been

funny to see.

When Mrs. Kerr was a girl she lived on a farm
in Missouri. One spring day, she found a baby
duck. Mrs. Kerr named it Webster. She kept
Webster for a pet. Mrs. Kerr also had a dog
named Wags. Wags liked Webster. He let the
duckling sit on his back. In the summer, Mrs.
Kerr, Webster, and Wags went swimming at Blue
Lake. They must have been funny to see.

_____

_____

Capitalization—Proper Nouns

Read the story and circle each noun that should begin with a capital letter. Write the noun correctly above the circle. Then write the story correctly on the lines below.

Mario was a member of the (lakeshore) [Lakeshore] Reading Club. The club

wanted to have a fundraiser to help support the (elm) [Elm] Street Library.

Mario asked Mr. (matlock) [Matlock] for advice on planning a fundraiser. Mr.

(matlock) [Matlock] suggested that the club sponsor a car wash. Mario asked Mrs.

(wilson,) [Wilson] owner of (wilson's groceries,) [Wilson's Groceries] if the club could host the car wash

in the store parking lot. She agreed, and the (lakeshore reading club) [Lakeshore Reading Club] had

its first fundraiser car wash.

Mario was a member of the Lakeshore

Reading Club. The club wanted to have a

fundraiser to help support the Elm Street Library.

Mario asked Mr. Matlock for advice on planning a

fundraiser. Mr. Matlock suggested that the club

sponsor a car wash. Mario asked Mrs. Wilson,

owner of Wilson's Groceries, if the club could

host the car wash in the store parking lot. She

agreed, and the Lakeshore Reading Club had its

first fundraiser car wash.

Name_____ Date_____

Capitalization—Dates and Holidays

Read the following sentences and circle each noun that should begin with a capital letter. Write the noun correctly above the circle. Then write the sentences correctly on the lines below.

1. Melanie's birthday is in (march,) and mine is in (august.)
   March   August

   Melanie's birthday is in March, and mine is in

   August.

2. We celebrate (thanksgiving) on the fourth (thursday) in (november.)
   Thanksgiving   Thursday   November

   We celebrate Thanksgiving on the fourth

   Thursday in November.

3. The (fourth) of (july) is (rachel's) favorite holiday.
   Fourth July Rachel's

   The Fourth of July is Rachel's favorite holiday.

4. For (memorial day) we are having a picnic.
   Memorial Day

   For Memorial Day we are having a picnic.

5. Pete's vacation begins on (friday, july) 5.
   Friday, July

   Pete's vacation begins on Friday, July 5.

6. My grandparents lived through the (great depression.)
   Great Depression

   My grandparents lived through the Great

   Depression.

UNIT 5   Storytelling • **Lesson 6** *Johnny Appleseed*

Capitalization—Dates and Holidays

Read the following sentences and circle each noun that should begin with a capital letter. Write the noun correctly above the circle. Then write the sentences correctly on the lines below.

1. The(civil war)is an important part of(american)history.
   Civil War   American

   <u>The Civil War is an important part of American</u>

   <u>history.</u>

2. Juanita's birthday is on(tuesday, april)22.
   Tuesday, April

   <u>Juanita's birthday is on Tuesday, April 22.</u>

3. The(valentine's day)party is at(shaw elementary school.)
   Valentine's Day   Shaw Elementary School

   <u>The Valentine's Day party is at Shaw</u>

   <u>Elementary School.</u>

4. Mica and(kyle)are doing a report about(world war I.)
              Kyle   World War I

   <u>Mica and Kyle are doing a report about</u>

   <u>World War I.</u>

5. (june, july,)and(august)are favorite months for vacations.
   June, July   August

   <u>June, July, and August are favorite months for</u>

   <u>vacations.</u>

6. My dentist appointment is on(wednesday, january)6.
                               Wednesday, January

   <u>My dentist appointment is on Wednesday,</u>

   <u>January 6.</u>

UNIT 5   Storytelling • **Lesson 6** *Johnny Appleseed*

Capitalization—Dates and Holidays

Read the following sentences and circle each noun that should begin with a capital letter. Write the noun correctly above the circle. Then write the sentences correctly on the lines below.

Labor Day   Hoover Park
1. The (labor day) celebration is at (hoover park.)

   The Labor Day celebration is at Hoover Park.

   March
2. (march) 12 is the date Sheila returns from vacation.

   March 12 is the date Sheila returns from vacation.

   August
3. The new library will open in (august.)

   The new library will open in August.

   Tuesdays   Thursdays
4. I have soccer practice on (tuesdays) and (thursdays.)

   I have soccer practice on Tuesdays and Thursdays.

   February
5. The car has been broken since (february.)

   The car has been broken since February.

   Saturday
6. Our family goes out together every (saturday.)

   Our family goes out together every Saturday.

Name_____ Date _____

Conjunctions and Compound Sentences

Read the story. The wrong words are used to combine the sentences. Circle each word that is wrong and add a comma, if necessary. Write the comma and correct word above the circle. Then write the story correctly on the lines below.

, and

Stan got a basket (or) he put it on the counter. Anna made

, and   , and

sandwiches (but) she put them in the basket. Tommy made lemonade (but)

, and

he put it in the cooler. Mom made brownies (or) she cut up some carrots,

, but

too. They helped Dad pack the car (and) they were not quite ready. Would

, or

they go to Kent Park (but) would they visit Big Woods? They talked about

, and   , and

where to go (or) they voted. Big Woods won (or) now they were ready.

    Stan got a basket, and he put it on the counter.

Anna made sandwiches, and she put them in the

basket. Tommy made lemonade, and he put it in

the cooler. Mom made brownies, and she cut up

some carrots, too. They helped Dad pack the car,

but they were not quite ready. Would they go to

Kent Park, or would they visit Big Woods? They

talked about where to go, and they voted. Big

Woods won, and now they were ready.

_____

Conjunctions and Compound Sentences

Read the story. The wrong words are used to combine the sentences. Circle each word that is wrong and add a comma, if necessary. Write the comma and correct word above the circle. Then write the story correctly on the lines below.

, and

Nan and her mom will go camping (but) they will go fishing, too.

, and

They pack a tent (or) they pack camping gear. They pack fishing poles

, and

(but) they also pack hooks and bait. Nan and her mom may camp in a

, or   , and

campground (and) they may camp in a park. Nan likes to hike (or) she likes

, but

to swim. The campground has a pool (and) it has no place to hike. For

fishing, a pool won't work, so where should they go?

 Nan and her mom will go camping, and they
will go fishing, too. They pack a tent, and they
pack camping gear. They pack fishing poles, and
they also pack hooks and bait. Nan and her mom
may camp in a campground, or they may camp in
a park. Nan likes to hike, and she likes to swim.
The campground has a pool, but it has no place
to hike. For fishing, a pool won't work, so where
should they go?

Conjunctions and Compound Sentences

Read the story. Some of these sentences can be combined. Put an arrow where a comma and conjunction should be inserted. Then write the story correctly on the lines below.

Doug lives in Chicago. His best friend, Bill, lives in Cleveland. Doug moved one year ago. The two friends haven't seen each other since then. Doug would like to see his friend again. He has asked his parents what to do. They said he could invite his friend and his parents to come for a visit. That's what he did. Bill and his family will visit next month.

__Answers may vary.__

__Doug lives in Chicago, but his best friend, Bill, lives in Cleveland. Doug moved one year ago, and the two friends haven't seen each other since then. Doug would like to see his friend again, and he has asked his parents what to do. They said he could invite his friend and his parents to come for a visit, and that's what he did. Bill and his family will visit next month.__

_____

_____

Commas in a Series

Read the story. Place an arrow where each comma should be added. Put a comma above each arrow. Then write the story correctly on the lines below.

Phil͵Jim͵and Mary wanted to donate money to the food drive. They thought about selling lemonade͵cookies͵or popcorn. They decided to have a lemonade stand. They went to the store and got lemons͵sugar͵and ice. Phil's mom donated cups͵pitchers͵and a sign. Many people stopped͵bought͵and drank lemonade. The children made ten dollars from the stand. Phil͵ Jim͵and Mary gave all the money they earned to the food drive.

Phil, Jim, and Mary, wanted to donate money to the food drive. They thought about selling lemonade, cookies, or popcorn. They decided to have a lemonade stand. They went to the store and got lemons, sugar, and ice. Phil's mom donated cups, pitchers, and a sign. Many people stopped, bought, and drank lemonade. The children made ten dollars from the stand. Phil, Jim, and Mary gave all the money they earned to the food drive.

Name_____ Date_____

Commas in a Series

Read the story. Place an arrow where each comma should be added. Put a comma above each arrow. Then write the story correctly on the lines below.

Lisa Beth and Terri were going to have a party for their teacher, Miss Oliver. Lisa made special invitations for everyone in the class. Beth was in charge of decorations. She used signs streamers and balloons. Terri brought punch brownies and candy for the party. Everyone had a great time. They all laughed played games and sang songs. Lisa Beth and Terri were glad that they planned organized and created such a wonderful surprise.

Lisa, Beth, and Terri were going to have a party for their teacher, Miss Oliver. Lisa made special invitations for everyone in the class. Beth was in charge of decorations. She used signs, streamers, and balloons. Terri brought punch, brownies, and candy for the party. Everyone had a great time. They all laughed, played games, and sang songs. Lisa, Beth, and Terri were glad that they planned, organized, and created such a wonderful surprise.

UNIT 6 Country Life • **Lesson I** *The Country Mouse and the City Mouse*

Commas in a Series

Read the story. Place an arrow where each comma should be added. Put a comma above each arrow. Then write the story correctly on the lines below.

Luis was going to visit his grandparents for the weekend. He loved to stay there because they always had fun games, delicious food, and special treats. Sometimes when he stayed they would go to the zoo, park, or a movie. When they stayed indoors they would read stories, play games, or prepare food together. This weekend his cousins Hector, Carla, and Jorge were going to be there as well. He thought they would have lots of fun together.

Luis was going to visit his grandparents for the weekend. He loved to stay there because they always had fun games, delicious food, and special treats. Sometimes when he stayed they would go to the zoo, park, or a movie. When they stayed indoors they would read stories, play games, or prepare food together. This weekend his cousins Hector, Carla, and Jorge were going to be there as well. He thought they would have lots of fun together.

UNIT 6 Country Life • **Lesson 2** *Heartland*

Apostrophes—Possessive Nouns

Read the story and circle each noun that needs an apostrophe. Then write the story correctly on the lines below.

(Tims) family went to the zoo. Tim liked all the (tigers) stripes. He was surprised at each (giraffes) long neck. He watched a zookeeper toss the seals some food. His one (sisters) favorite animal was the chimp. The (chimps) name was Toto. (Totos) cage had a tree and some toys. Toto swung on the (trees) branches. He also played with his toys.

Tim's family went to the zoo. Tim liked all the tigers' stripes. He was surprised at each giraffe's long neck. He watched a zookeeper toss the seals some food. His one sister's favorite animal was the chimp. The chimp's name was Toto. Toto's cage had a tree and some toys. Toto swung on the tree's branches. He also played with his toys.

_____

_____

_____

_____

Apostrophes—Possessive Nouns

**Read the story and circle each noun that needs an apostrophe.
Then write the story correctly on the lines below.**

Mr. (Clarks) class had a bake sale. (Jims) mom made a cake. (Macks) dad baked cupcakes. The Barton (brothers) sister made brownies. (Juans) brother made cookies. They had a table piled with treats.

The children put the table by the (principals) office. They sold (everyones) treats. Juan counted the (groups) money. The class would buy a tree. They would plant the tree in the (schools) yard.

Mr. Clark's class had a bake sale. Jim's mom made a cake. Mack's dad baked cupcakes. The Barton brothers' sister made brownies. Juan's brother made cookies. They had a table piled with treats.

The children put the table by the principal's office. They sold everyone's treats. Juan counted the group's money. The class would buy a tree. They would plant the tree in the school's yard.

_____

_____

UNIT 6   Country Life • **Lesson 2** *Heartland*

Apostrophes—Possessive Nouns

Read the story and circle each noun that needs an apostrophe. Then write the story correctly on the lines below.

Karen has many books. (Karens) favorite book right now is a story about Poco the puppy. She has another book about a (gorillas) family. Karen keeps some of her books at her (grandparents) house. Her one (sisters) and one (brothers) books are there as well. They often read stories to each other when they stay at their house.

Karen has many books. Karen's favorite book right now is a story about Poco the puppy. She has another book about a gorilla's family. Karen keeps some of her books at her grandparent's house. Her one sister's and one brother's books are there as well. They often read stories to each other when they stay at their house.

_____

_____

_____

_____

Name_____ Date_____

Sentence Types

Read the story and insert the correct end mark at the end of each sentence. Then write the story correctly on the lines below.

Do you have a scrapbook? It's a great way to remember things you did. You can put in photos, postcards, or even pictures you draw. Do you like to write? You can write on the pages. You can even add stickers!

It's fun to look at the pages in your scrapbook. You can also share it with your friends. Who else do you think might like to see it? Don't forget to share it with your family.

__Do you have a scrapbook? It's a great way to__
__remember things you did. You can put in photos,__
__postcards, or even pictures you draw. Do you like__
__to write? You can write on the pages. You can__
__even add stickers!__
__It's fun to look at the pages in your scrapbook.__
__You can also share it with your friends. Who else__
__do you think might like to see it? Don't forget to__
__share it with your family.__

_____

_____

UNIT 6   Country Life • **Lesson 3** *Leah's Pony*

Sentence Types

Read the story and insert the correct end mark at the end of each sentence. Then write the story correctly on the lines below.

Have you ever visited a farm? Most farms grow crops, but they also have different kinds of animals. They usually have some cows and some chickens. Often they have horses and sheep. Many have dogs and cats.

Some farm animals have jobs to do. Chickens lay eggs for the farmer and his family. Cows give their milk. Horses can be ridden all over the farm. Sheep provide wool that can be made into yarn for sweaters. Can you think of any other farm animals and the jobs they do?

Have you ever visited a farm? Most farms grow crops, but they also have different kinds of animals. They usually have some cows and some chickens. Often they have horses and sheep. Many have dogs and cats.

Some farm animals have jobs to do. Chickens lay eggs for the farmer and his family. Cows give their milk. Horses can be ridden all over the farm. Sheep provide wool that can be made into yarn for sweaters. Can you think of any other farm animals and the jobs they do?

UNIT 6 Country Life • **Lesson 3** *Leah's Pony*

Sentence Types

Read the sentences and add the correct end mark to each sentence.

1. What a beautiful day it is**!**

2. Where are you going**?**

3. This is my favorite place to go fishing**.**

4. Would you like to go with me**?**

5. You are so lucky**!**

Follow the prompts to write your own sentences.

Write a statement.

1. <u>Answers will vary.</u>

_____

Write a question.

2. <u>Answers will vary.</u>

_____

Write an exclamation.

3. <u>Answers will vary.</u>

_____

UNIT 6   Country Life • **Lesson 4**   *Cows in the Parlor: A Visit to a Dairy Farm*

Exclamation and Question Marks

Read the following sentences and add the correct end punctuation mark to each one. Then copy the sentences correctly on the lines below. Be careful, some of the sentences are statements and some are exclamations.

1. Does anyone know what time it is?

   Does anyone know what time it is? _____

2. What an exciting game!

   What an exciting game! _____

3. This book is very good.

   This book is very good. _____

4. My mother is visiting her sister.

   My mother is visiting her sister. _____

5. Will you help me do my homework?

   Will you help me do my homework? _____

6. Shh, it's too noisy!

   Shh, it's too noisy! _____

UNIT 6 Country Life • **Lesson 4** *Cows in the Parlor: A Visit to a Dairy Farm*

Exclamation and Question Marks

Read the following sentences and add the correct end punctuation mark to each one. Then copy the sentences correctly on the lines below. Be careful, some of the sentences are statements and some are exclamations.

1. Do you know the answer to my question?

   Do you know the answer to my question?_____

2. Try some apple pie.

   Try some apple pie._____

3. Stop yelling!

   Stop yelling!_____

4. Does Martha know Spanish?

   Does Martha know Spanish?_____

5. What a great surprise!

   What a great surprise!_____

6. Rick painted the house last weekend.

   Rick painted the house last weekend._____

UNIT 6   Country Life • **Lesson 4** *Cows in the Parlor: A Visit to a Dairy Farm*

Exclamation and Question Marks

Read the following sentences and add the correct end punctuation mark to each one. Then copy the sentences correctly on the lines below.

1. What a beautiful painting!

   What a beautiful painting!

2. Have you seen my library card?

   Have you seen my library card?

3. Who made this delicious cake?

   Who made this delicious cake?

4. You won't believe what I just saw!

   You won't believe what I just saw!

5. Which one of these is yours?

   Which one of these is yours?

6. Can you help me answer the question?

   Can you help me answer the question?

Follow the prompts to write your own sentences.

Write a question.

7. **Answers will vary.**

Write an exclamation.

8. **Answers will vary.**

Name_____ Date_____

Verb Tenses

Read the story. Choose a verb from the following list to complete each sentence. Fill in the blanks with the correct verbs.

learned	saw	went	wait
want	will	are	see

Tomorrow, Tad and Mandy _____**will**_____ go to the Native

American museum. They _____**went**_____ last year. They

_____**saw**_____ many pieces of jewelry and other crafts. This year

they _____**want**_____ to see Native American villages. They already

_____**learned**_____ about different villages in school. The museum has

several tepees. Tad and Mandy _____**are**_____ excited about the trip.

They know they will _____**see**_____ many things. They can hardly

_____**wait**_____ for tomorrow.

UNIT 6 Country Life • **Lesson 5** *Just Plain Fancy*

Verb Tenses

Read the story. Choose a verb from the following list to complete each sentence. Fill in the blanks with the correct verbs.

spending   won   is   been   be

eat   stay   taking   found

This has ____**been**____ a great week for Emma. On Monday, she

____**found**____ her lost box of paints. Tuesday she ____**won**____

the Spelling Bee. Today, Emma's mom is ____**taking**____ her for ice

cream after school. That will ____**be**____ fun! On Friday, Emma

will be ____**spending**____ the night with her best friend, Grace. They will

____**eat**____ popcorn and ____**stay**____ up late. This really

____**is**____ Emma's lucky week.

Name_____ Date_____

Verb Tenses

Read the sentences and circle the correct verb form.

1. Manuel and Tim (will go, went) to the park tonight.

2. Yesterday I (help, helped) my mom do the dishes.

3. Kittens (were, are) cute and playful.

4. Last year, Harry (goes, went) to his aunt's house every day after school.

5. The people we met on vacation last year (were, will be) very friendly.

Follow the prompts to write your own sentences.

Write a sentence with a past tense verb.

1. <u>Answers will vary.</u>

_____

Write a sentence with a present tense verb.

2. <u>Answers will vary.</u>

_____

Write a sentence with a future tense verb.

3. <u>Answers will vary.</u>

_____

UNIT 6 Country Life • **Lesson 6** *What Ever Happened to the Baxter Place?*

Subject-Verb Agreement

Read the story and circle each incorrect verb. Write the correct verb over each circle. Then write the story correctly on the lines below.

         walk   pass

Zoe and I (walks) to the bus stop every morning. We (passes) Mr.

has   comes

Carr's farm. He (have) a pony named Rex. Rex (come) to the fence when

              likes   give   pet

we walk by. I know that Rex (like) apples. We (gives) him an apple and (pets)

                                    wave

him. Then we meet our friends at the bus stop. They (waves) to us. We

tell   wait

(tells) them about Rex. Then we (waits) for Mrs. Stone, our bus driver. She

is

(are) always on time.

_____Zoe and I walk to the bus stop every morning._

We pass Mr. Carr's farm. He has a pony named

Rex. Rex comes to the fence when we walk by. I

know that Rex likes apples. We give him an apple

and pet him. Then we meet our friends at the bus

stop. They wave to us. We tell them about Rex.

Then we wait for Mrs. Stone, our bus driver. She

is always on time.

_____

_____

Subject-Verb Agreement

Read the story and circle each incorrect verb. Write the correct verb over each circle. Then write the story correctly on the lines below.

work

Steve and Carrie (works) in Mrs. Smith's yard. Steve's job (are) to

is

cleans   finds

sweep her walk. Carrie (clean) out the doghouse. She (find) Spot's ball. The

was

ball (were) in the bushes. When Steve and Carrie finish, Mrs. Smith's yard

looks   gives

(look) very nice. She (give) each child a dollar for their hard work. Then,

asks   help

she (ask) them to come back next week and (helps) again. Steve and Carrie

are

(is) excited about their new jobs.

Steve and Carrie work in Mrs. Smith's yard.
Steve's job is to sweep her walk. Carrie cleans
out the doghouse. She finds Spot's ball. The
ball was in the bushes. When Steve and Carrie
finish, Mrs. Smith's yard looks very nice. She
gives each child a dollar for their hard work.
Then, she asks them to come back next week
and help again. Steve and Carrie are excited
about their new jobs.

Name_____ Date _____

Subject-Verb Agreement

Read the story and circle each incorrect verb. Write the correct verb over each circle. Then write the story correctly on the lines below.

Shana and her family are going to the country for the weekend.

go

They (goes) often to stay with Shana's aunt and uncle. Her aunt and uncle

live   have

(lives) on a farm. They (has) horses, cows, sheep, and chickens. When

is   helps   feeds

Shana (are) there, she (help) take care of the animals. She (feed) them and

likes

cleans the stalls. She (like) the horses best. Sometimes, she even gets to

ride one in the pasture.

___Shana and her family are going to the country___

___for the weekend. They go often to stay with___

___Shana's aunt and uncle. Her aunt and uncle live___

___on a farm. They have horses, cows, sheep, and___

___chickens. When Shana is there, she helps take___

___care of the animals. She feeds them and cleans___

___the stalls. She likes the horses best. Sometimes,___

___she even gets to ride one in the pasture.___

_____

_____

Capitalization

Read the story and circle each word that should be capitalized. Then copy the story correctly on the lines below.

(megan's) dog, (queenie,) is a collie. (she) has four little puppies. (they) look like cuddly balls of fur. (megan) handles them gently. (they) are just babies. (she) likes to watch them stumble over each other. (they) wiggle and waggle when (megan) holds them.

Megan's dog, Queenie, is a collie. She has four

little puppies. They look like cuddly balls of fur.

Megan handles them gently. They are just babies.

She likes to watch them stumble over each other.

They wiggle and waggle when Megan holds

_them._____

_____

_____

_____

_____

_____

_____

Capitalization

Read the story and circle each word that should be capitalized. Then copy the story correctly on the lines below.

(kim) was filled with sadness when her family left (cityville) (all) she could think about was the friendliness of her old classmates. (now) (kim) had to go to (town) (school) (she) worried no one would like her. (kim) was not careful as she walked. (she) tripped and dropped her backpack. (a) girl named (sue) stopped and helped her. (kim) was grateful for (sue's) help. (sue) was in (kim's) new class. (they) quickly became friends.

<u>   Kim was filled with sadness when her family</u>
<u>left Cityville. All she could think about was the</u>
<u>friendliness of her old classmates. Now Kim had</u>
<u>to go to Town School. She worried no one would</u>
<u>like her. Kim was not careful as she walked. She</u>
<u>tripped and dropped her backpack. A girl named</u>
<u>Sue stopped and helped her. Kim was grateful for</u>
<u>Sue's help. Sue was in Kim's new class. They</u>
<u>quickly became friends.</u>
_____
_____

UNIT 6   Country Life • **Lesson 7** *If you're not from the prairie*

Capitalization

**Read the story and circle each word that should be capitalized.
Then copy the story correctly on the lines below.**

(bill) and (nick) are brothers. (they) had always lived in the country.
(this) year their family moved to (chicago.) (at) first (nick) and (bill) did not
think they would like the city. (then) they learned how to get around the
city on the trains and buses. (now) they can go to the park or the library
on their own. (when) their cousins come to visit, (nick) and (bill) like
showing them the places in the city that they like. Nick and Bill really
enjoy living in (chicago.)

_____Bill and Nick are brothers. They had always_____

lived in the country. This year their family moved

to Chicago. At first Nick and Bill did not think

they would like the city. Then they learned how to

get around the city on the trains and buses. Now

they can go to the park or the library on their own.

When their cousins come to visit, Nick and Bill

like showing them the places in the city that they

like. Nick and Bill really enjoy living in Chicago.

_____

Intervention   UNIT 6 • Lesson 7   Worksheet **107**